A Practical Manual
on
GEOLOGY AND SOILS

About the Author

Dr. A. S. Mailappa, Associate Professor (Soil Science and Agrl. Chemistry), College of Horticulture and Forestry, Central Agricultural University (Imphal), Pasighat, Arunachal Pradesh, obtained his M.Sc.(Ag.) in Soil Science and Agricultural Chemistry in 2000 from University of Agricultural Sciences (UAS, Bengaluru) under ICAR – Junior Research Fellowship and Ph.D. from Tamil Nadu Agricultural University (TNAU, Coimbatore) in 2003 under Neyveli Lignite Corporation (NLC) Senior Research Fellowship. He was working as JRF and SRF (Junior & Senior Research Fellow) in various projects including Indian Space Research Organization (ISRO) during November, 1998 to March, 2007. He joined as Assistant Professor (Soil Science and Agrl. Chemistry) in College of Agriculture, Lembucherra, Tripura, during August, 2007 and in College of Horticulture and Forestry, Central Agricultural University (Imphal), Pasighat, Arunachal Pradesh, during September, 2009. In addition, he assumed the responsibility as Scientist In-charge (Soil Health Card Scheme) from October 2015 and Principal Investigator & Chief Executive Officer (CEO) of RKVY-RAFTAAR Agribusiness Incubator since March, 2019. He is specialized in Soil Chemistry, Soil Fertility and has Soil Microbiology and has published more than 20 research papers in reputed journals, 7 books, 37 book chapters and several practical manuals & technical bulletins. He received several prestigious awards for his immense contribution to Teaching, Research and Extension including Best Krishi Shikshak Award (Best Academician Award), Scientist Award – 2019 (Dr.B.V.David Foundation), Excellence in Teaching Award (SVWS), Excellence in Research Award (DRASS), Best Scientist Award (SFSN), Excellence in Innovation Award – 2020 (Dr. B.V. David Foundation) and guided many PG and Ph.D students. His significant contributions are establishment of RKVY- RAFTAAR Agri Business Innovation Hub for promoting entrepreneurship in Agriculture / Horticulture and allied sectors, development of reclamation and management measures and nutrient management strategies for acid soils of North Eastern Hilly Region of India, detailed investigation on dynamics of potassium in acid soils of Arunachal Pradesh, study of carbon sequestration potential in horti-silvipastural systems and delineation of organic carbon and organic matter content of acid soils of Arunachal Pradesh. As a whole, he has made commendable contribution in Teaching, Research and Extension towards the development of Agriculture and Horticulture in the North Eastern Hilly Region of India.

A Practical Manual on GEOLOGY AND SOILS

A.S. Mailappa
Associate Professor (Soil Science and Agricultural Chemistry)
College of Horticulture and Forestry
Central Agricultural University (Imphal)
Passighat, Arunachal Pradesh, India

NEW INDIA PUBLISHING AGENCY
New Delhi – 110 034

NEW INDIA PUBLISHING AGENCY
101, Vikas Surya Plaza, CU Block, LSC Market
Pitam Pura, New Delhi - 110 034, India
Email: info@nipabooks.com
Web: www.nipabooks.com

For customer assistance, please contact
Phone: + 91-11-27 34 17 17 Fax: + 91-11- 27 34 16 16
E-mail: feedbacks@nipabooks.com

ISBN : 978-81-94766-83-4

Composed and Designed by NIPA.

Dedicated to
My Beloved Students

केन्द्रीय कृषि विश्वविद्यालय
लम्फेलपात, इम्फाल–795004, मणिपुर (भारत)

CENTRAL AGRICULTURAL UNIVERSITY

LAMPHELPAT, IMPHAL-795004, MANIPUR (INDIA)

Tel: + 91 - 9582898989
Email: sayyappan1955@gmail.com
Resi: 106, Sankalp Basant, # 40 & 41, Akkamahadevi Road, Industrial Suburb, Mysuru South, Mysuru-570008, Karnataka, India

Prof. S. Ayyappan
Chancellor

Foreword

In the changing scenario of a comprehensive, vibrant and quality agricultural education system, in congruence with a dynamic research and technology developing setting, the urgency for strengthening our educational standard, graduates' employability, and research and extension outcomes can hardly be over emphasized. The Fifth Deans' Committee, underpinning the congruence of excellence and relevance, has judiciously updated the curricula, course contents, and degree nomenclature, and recommended reforms in admission and examination, pedagogy, faculty requirement, governance, etc.

While addressing the academic legitimacy of new and emerging issues of food and agriculture systems, the students need to update their professional calibre and employability skills to sustain the competitive market. Considering various difficulties and work-pressure faced by the students to cope up the changing scenario of agricultural education, there is an urgent need of providing easy online & offline access of content/ study materials of various courses to the students.

In this context, this book entitled 'A Practical Manual on Geology and Soils', prepared by Dr A. S. Mailappa, Associate Professor (Soil Science and Agricultural Chemistry), College of Horticulture & Forestry, Pasighat, Arunachal Pradesh, CAU, Imphal, is an outcome of his visionary perception and quest of a great need for an easy ready reckoner practical manual for the undergraduate students of Agriculture, Horticulture and Forestry in particular and scientific community related to the domain of Agriculture in general. It is an authentic treatise and written in such a way that the reader shall easily understand various practical aspects of geology and soils in 25 well-defined chapters. At the end of every chapter, the author has also placed some questions, igniting the minds of readers to have in-depth understanding of the subject.

I am confident that the book will be very useful for the undergraduate and post graduate students, researchers, and an important addition to the university library. The book deserves to be a standard practical manual of geology and soils in colleges and universities.

(S. Ayyappan)
27th November 2020

Preface

"Soil - The Soul of Infinite Life" a acronym is more than sufficient to highlight the importance of soil. Soil is the great connector of our lives, the source and destination of all. It is the healer, restorer of everything that supports our life on this planet. Without proper care for it, we can have no life on this planet.

The importance of soil and soil management is being increasingly recognized in our country. Which have a high pressure of population on the available land and find no alternative in meeting the demand for food and other agricultural raw materials except through increase in agricultural production per unit land.

Soil Science is a unique discipline concerning a complex material that is part of many natural and utilitarian systems. Geology is the applied discipline of science and is now established as an interdisciplinary subject within agriculture, soil and environmental science as the agriculturists and soil /environmental scientists heavily require geological knowledge and information to apply in the field. As such, a basic reference practical manual is highly needed for anyone to understand the practical aspects of geology and soils that ultimately help to understand the nature and properties of soil and its relation to plant growth.

This book is an outcome of my visionary perception and quest of a great need for an easy ready reckoner cum reference practical manual on geology and soils for the undergraduate students of Agriculture, Horticulture and Forestry.

Utilizing my decade-long academic & professional experience and conception on practical aspects of geology and soils, this book is written in a very simpler and lucid manner, following the syllabi of latest Fifth Deans' Committee for undergraduate programmes being followed in various Agricultural Universities in India, to ensure easy and clear understanding about various spheres of geology and soil science.

This book is primarily intended for the students and scientists of associated with agriculture and allied disciplines, for having a better understanding about 'practical geology and soil science', a prerequisite for progressing ahead in acquiring in-depth knowledge on the application aspects of soil science in relation to crop growth.

I hope that this book entitled "A Practical Manual on Geology and Soils" will meet the requirement of all the undergraduate and postgraduate students of soil science and other disciplines related to agriculture, horticulture and forestry and inspire them to expand their ideas and horizons in all possible ways.

Finally, I take this opportunity to express my sincere and heartfelt regards with deep sense of gratitude to our honourable Vice Chancellor Dr. Anupam Mishra, Central Agricultural University, Imphal for his visionary guidance and imperative efforts in aligning and contextualising the academic pursuits with contemporary and projected national and global agricultural trends. The author is also very much grateful to Dr.S.Basanta Singh, Director of Instruction, Central Agricultural University, Imphal and Dr. B.N. Hazarika, Dean, College of Horticulture and Forestry, for their constant encouragement and meticulous support for bringing out of this book.

A. S. Mailappa
26th Nov, 2020

Contents

1

Analytical Chemistry - Basic Concepts

Analytical chemistry is a branch of chemistry dealing with the determination of constituents of a substance or mixture of substances.

1.1 Qualitative Analysis

Qualitative analysis deals with the identification of the constituents of a substance, mixture of substances, or solutions and the way in which component element or a group of elements are constituted.

1.2 Quantitative Analysis

Quantitative analysis is concerned with the determination of quantitative contents of individual element or group of elements or compound present in the substances. This branch of analytical chemistry is of enormous scope and importance in science, industry and agriculture. The quantitative analysis can be divided into several categories based on the different methods employed for their quantitative measurements such as:

- Volumetric Analysis or Titrimetric Analysis
- Gravimetric Analysis
- Electro Gravimetric Analysis
- Electro Volumetric (Potentiometric / Conductometric) Analysis
- Polorographic Analysis
- Colorimetric Analysis
- Nephelometric or Turbidometric Analysis
- Chromatographic Analysis
- Radiometric Analysis

1.3 Basic Principles in Analytical Chemistry

A general conception of important fundamentals is essential in analytical chemistry. Number of important principles and definitions are involved in Quantitative Analysis.

1.3.1 Mass and Weight

The mass of a substance is a definite property which can be used as a measure of quantity. The weight of the substance is the force which results from the interaction of the gravitational field on the substance.

Mass can be determined with the help of balance whereas weight should actually be used to express force.

1.3.2 Atom and Atomic Weight

Atom is the smallest particle of an element, which retains its property and takes part in chemical reaction. Atomic weight is the average weight of an element relative to weight of carbon atom as 12. The unit of atomic weight of an element is a.m.u. $atom^{-1}$ (atomic mass unit per atom). The atomic weight expressed in grams is known as gram atom. e.g. 16 g of oxygen means one gram atom of oxygen.

1.3.3 Molecule and Molecular Weight

Molecule is the smallest particle of substance (element/compound) which retains the property of that substance and exists in free state.

Molecular weight of a substance is defined as the weight of one molecule of the substance relative to the weight of carbon atom as 12. The molecular weight is sum of the atomic weights of the elements present in one molecule of the substance. When molecular weight is expressed in grams, it is termed as gram molecule or mole. e.g. 32 grams of oxygen means one gram molecule or one mole of oxygen.

1.3.4 Avogadro's Number

The actual number of molecules present in one mole of substance is known as Avogadro's number and has the value of 6.024×10^{23}. Thus one mole of every substance contains 6.024×10^{23} molecules. This quantity also expresses the number of atoms in one gram atom of an element and hence 1 gram atom of every element contains 6.024×10^{23} atoms.

1.3.5 Equivalent Weight

The equivalent weight of a substance is defined as the weight of an element or compound which combines with or displaces from combination, 8 parts by weight of oxygen or 1.008 parts by weight of hydrogen or 35.5 parts by weight of chlorine. The equivalent weight expressed in grams is termed as gram equivalent weight.

1.3.6 Standard Solutions

The solution of accurately known strength or concentration is called as a standard solution. It contains a definite number of gram equivalent or gram mole per litre of the solution.

1.3.7 Strength or Concentration of a solution

Strength of a solution refers to the weight of a solute dissolved in one litre or per unit volume of the solution. It can be expressed in many ways.

1.3.8 Normal Solution or Normality

A normal solution is one which contain one gram equivalent (equivalent weight in grams) of the active reagent, dissolved in one litre of solution.

Normality is the number of gram equivalent of substance, dissolved in one litre of solution. If the number of gram equivalent is one, it is expressed as 1 ***N***. Normality = Number of gram equivalent of solute / Number of litres per solution

1.3.9 Molar Solution or Molarity

A molar solution is one which contains a gram molecular weight of solute dissolved in one litre of solution. It is denoted by M, whereas Molarity is the number of gram molecule of substance dissolved in one litre of solution.

1.3.10 Molal Solution

A Molal solution is one which contains a number of gram molecules of the solute dissolved in 1000 g of solvent.

1.3.11 Mole Fraction

It is defined as the ratio of the number of moles of solute to the number of moles of solution.

1.3.12 Formal Solution

A formal solution is one which contains a formula weight of a solute in a litre of solution and is denoted by **F**. In most of the cases, formula weight and molecular weight are identical but sometimes the true molecular weight of a compound is a multiple of the weight expressed by its formula as ordinarily written in a chemical reaction.

1.3.13 Percentage Composition by Weight

The concentration is expressed in terms of grams of solute per 100 grams of solution. For instance, a 10 % KI solution is prepared by dissolving 10 grams of the salt in 90 grams of water.

1.3.14 Strength or Percentage Strength

Strength of a solution means the grams of solute or substance dissolved in one litre of solution and usually expressed as g/litre. Percentage strength means the grams of solute per 100 mL of solution.

1.3.15 Parts per million (ppm)

The concentration is expressed in terms of grams of solute per milliliters of solution or milligrams of solute per litre of solution. Thus, a solution containing 10 mg of solute per litre of solution or 10 microgram of solute per millilitre of solution is 10 ppm solution.

1.3.16 Milli equivalent per litre

A solution containing milligram equivalent of substance in a litre of solution is called as Meq/litre.

1.3.17 Titration

Titration is defined as the process of determining the volume of a substance required to just complete the reaction with a known amount of other substances. The quantitative analysis carried out by titration is known as 'Titrimetric Analysis'.

1.3.18 Titrant

The solution of accurately known strength used in the titration is called as 'Titrant'.

1.3.19 Titrate

The substance (in solution) to be determined by titration is called as 'Titrate'.

1.3.20 Equivalence Point or End point

The point (in burette reading) at which the reaction is just complete in a titration is called the equivalence point or end point or stoichiometric end point. At this volume of Titrant, the reaction is completed quantitatively with a known volume of Titrate.

1.3.21 Indicators

A substance which indicates the end point or completion of reaction is called indicator. It is an auxiliary reagent which helps in the visual determination of the completion of titration. Indicators used commonly in volumetric analysis are of three types as follows:

1.3.22 Internal Indicators

The indicators added into the solution where reaction occurs is called internal indicator which gives a clear visual change (either a colour change or the formation of a turbidly) in the solution being titrated. Examples for internal indicators are:

1. Methyl Orange
2. Phenolphthalein
3. Methyl Red
4. Methylene Blue
5. Diphenylamine (DPA)

Internal indicators are divided into three groups according to their use in different types of reactions.

1.3.23 Indicators used in Acid- Alkali neutralization Reactions / Hydrogen ion / Acid-Base indicators

The hydrogen ion (acids-base) indicators are organic dyes (weak organic acids or bases) which changes colour within limits with variation in pH value of the solution to which it is added.

1. Methyl Orange
2. Phenolphthalein
3. Methyl Red
4. Bromothymol Blue
5. Phenol Red
6. Thymolpthalein

1.3.24 Indicators used in Precipitation Reactions

1. Potassium Chromate
2. Ferric Ammonium Alum

1.3.25 Indicators used in Oxidation-Reduction Reactions

1. Diphenylamine (DPA)
2. Methylene Blue
3. Eriochrome Black T (EBT)

1.3.26 External indicators

There are certain indicators which are not added to the reacting medium or kept away from the solution where reaction takes place are called as external indicators.

e.g. Potassium Ferricyanide

1.3.27 Self Indicator/Auto Indicator

When one of the reacting substances itself acts as indicator, by visual colour change is called self or auto indicator.

e.g. Potassium Permanganate

2

Laboratory Vessels and Their Uses

2.1 Beakers

- Beakers are the one of most important vessels used in laboratory which is made up of heat resistant glass.
- They are available in various capacities ranging from 10 to 3000 mL.
- For convenience of pouring solution, spout is provided in the beaker.
- They are used to perform titrations & for boiling solutions, etc.,
- Beakers are constructed in tall and low forms.

2.2 Pipettes

- Pipettes are used to deliver a definite volume precisely. They are of two kinds:
- Transfer or Volumetric pipette which delivers a definite volume of liquid under specified conditions.
- Graduated or Measuring pipettes in which the stems are graduated and are employed to deliver various small volumes at discretion.
- The transfer pipettes consists of a jet, a bulb and a tube bearing a mark.
- Sometimes, the pipettes are provided with a safety bulb above the mark.
- Transfer pipettes are constructed with capacities ranging from 1 to 100 mL (1, 2, 5, 10, 15, 20, 25, 50 and 100 mL) and are most frequently used in the work.
- Graduated pipettes are constructed with capacities ranging from 1 to 10 mL (1, 2, 5 and 10 mL).
- These are less précised than transfer pipettes.
- Micropipettes are also available and they are constructed with capacities ranging from 10 to 100 lamda (1 lamda = 0.001 mL).
- All these pipettes are calibrated to contain to deliver a definite volume of the solution in the given temperature usually 20°C to 30°C.

- In using such pipettes, they are first rinsed with the liquid and filled by suction to about 1 to 2 mL above the mark and the upper end of the pipette is closed with a dry index finger.
- By gently releasing the finger, the level of the solution may be brought to the point where the level of the meniscus coincides to the graduation mark on the pipette.
- The pipette thus filled will deliver exactly that volume of solution which is indicated on the bulb of the pipette.
- The solution is allowed to run out of pipette into a clean vessel.
- When the continuous flow has ceased, the jet is held in contact with the sides of the vessel for 15 seconds (draining time).
- At the end of the draining time, the tip of the pipette is removed from the contact.
- The liquid remaining in the jet of the pipette must not be removed either by blowing or by other means.
- Some pipettes are calibrated so that the liquid remaining in the jet can also be blown.
- Rubber bulbs are available for handling corrosive or toxic solutions.

2.3 Burettes

- Burettes are long of uniform bore throughout the graduated length terminating at the lower end in a glass cock and a jet.
- In cheaper varieties, a stop cock may be replaced by a pinch cock.
- The size varies from 10 to 100 mL (10, 20, 50 and 100 mL).
- The micro burette of 5 and 10 mL capacities are helpful in delivering volumes of 0.02 mL.
- Before use, the stop cock of the burette must be lubricated with vaseline.
- The burette is first rinsed with small quantities of Titrant solution.
- The burette is then filled to the mark slightly above the zero mark and the solution is made to run down so that the jet is free of air bubbles.
- Then the burette must be firmly attached to the stand.
- The liquid level is adjusted so that its lower level of meniscus coincides with zero level of the burette by using the stop cock.
- To deliver liquid from burette to vessel, place the fingers of the left hand behind the burette and hold the stop-cock between thumb, fore and middle fingers.

- During the delivery of the liquid, the flask may be gently rotated with the right hand to ensure that the added liquid is well mixed with any existing contents of the flask.

2.4 Graduated or Measuring Cylinders

- Measuring cylinders are graduated vessels with a broad base.
- They are used for approximate measurements of liquid and vary in size from 5 to 1000 mL.
- It is advisable to use the smallest cylinder that will hold the volume being measured.

2.5 Volumetric flasks

- It is a flat bottomed sphere vessel with a long narrow neck.
- A thin line marked around the neck indicates the volume that it holds.
- These are available in various sizes ranging from 5 to 2000 mL.
- A ground glass stopper is also provided with the flask.
- Volumetric flasks are used to prepare standard solutions.

2.6 Conical Flasks

- They are available in various capacities ranging from 50 to 1000 mL.
- They are very useful in performing titrations where the reactions are instantaneous.
- The narrow neck of the flask prevents the entry of external agencies like O_2, CO_2 etc., which sometimes may interfere with the analysis.

2.7 Funnels

- They are helpful for filtration and for transfer of liquids to narrow necked vessels.
- For filtration, the funnel should enclose an angle of 60°.
- The most useful size for titration is those with diameters of 5.75 and 9.00 cm.
- The stem should have an internal diameter of 4 cm and should not be > 15 cm long.
- For filling burettes and for transferring solids to volumetric flask, a short stemmed wide neck funnel is used.

2.8 Porcelain Crucibles and Basins

- These are employed for operations in which hot liquids are to remain in contact with vessels for prolonged period.
- They are usually more resistant to alkaline solutions than glass.
- They are also used for evaporating and concentrating the solutions.

2.9 Glass wash bottles and Polythene Squeeze Bottles

- They are useful to keep and deliver distilled water for various operations during analytical work.
- It is a necessary apparatus used to wash precipitate and rinse off the reagents from the glasswares.

2.10 Gooch Crucibles

- It is a porcelain crucible with perforated bottom.

2.11 Sintered Glass Crucibles

- They are made up of resistant glass and have a porous disc of sintered ground glass fused into the body.
- The filter disc is made of varying porosities as indicated by numbers from 0-5 (coarsest to finest).

2.12 Buckner Funnels

- They are made up of porcelain and fitted with a porous disc.
- One or two good quality filter papers are placed on the porous disc and filtration is done by suction.

2.13 Filter Flasks

- They are conical flasks fitted with a side vent, which can be attached to a vacuum pump to create vacuum in the conical flask during filtration.

2.14 Silica Basins and Crucibles

- They are used for ignition of precipitates.
- Advantages-It is resistant to heat & acids except hydrofluoric and phosphoric acid.
- Disadvantages-It is affected by alkali and carbonates and requires comparatively more time for heating and cooling.

2.15 Platinum Crucibles

- Platinum has high melting point (1773°C). Hence, they can be used for ignition of precipitates at high temperatures.

2.16 Desiccator

- It is a covered glass container designed for storage of objects in dry atmosphere.
- It is charged with some drying agents or desiccants like anhydrous calcium chloride, silica gel, activated alumina, anhydrous calcium sulphate and concentrated sulphuric acid.
- Hot crucibles are usually cooled inside a desiccator before weighing.

2.17 Miscellaneous Tools

- Miscellaneous tools are the supporting wares in the laboratory.
- They are burette stand, pipette stand, filter stand, tripod stand, wire gauze, clay pipe triangle, spatula, tongs, test tube holders, test tube stand, pestle and mortar, porcelain tiles etc.

2.18 Cleanness of Glasswares

- Cleanliness of the glasswares helps in a long way in improving the precision and accuracy of the analytical results.
- The glasswares are to be cleaned to sparking brightness to get rid of the contaminating radicals and other impurities.
- The glasswares may be washed initially in tap water to remove the soluble chemicals and dirt.
- To remove the greasy and water insoluble dirt and stains, hot detergent solutions preferably of 2 % strength may be of much helpful.
- The organic impurities and the hard to remove stains can be easily remove by using chemical mixture of commercial grade concentrated sulphuric acid with potassium dichromate salt. The chromic acid oxidizes the dirt and makes it easily removable.
- Sparking brightness of glasswares can be obtained by rinsing with commercial grade concentrated hydrochloric acid.
- After removal of dirt and stains, the wares should be washed free of detergent or acid particles with tap water, and finally a rinsing with small quantity of

distilled water may be given twice or thrice to remove the unwanted radicals which may come as a contamination from tap water.

- The washed glasswares may be stored in dust free environment after drying in hot air oven.

3

Basic Principles of Analytical Techniques and Instrumental Methods

Instrumental methods of chemical analysis are the quantitative methods of analysis that use, as principal measuring devices, instruments other than those employed in conventional gravimetric and volumetric determinations.

The main basis for this method of analysis is the physical property of any particular element or compound being analyzed. These properties include:

1. Mass/volume.
2. Specific gravity, surface tension, viscosity, velocity of sound.
3. Properties involving interaction with radiant energy-Absorption., scattering, emission.
4. Electric properties such as half cell potential, current voltage characteristics, electrical conductivity (EC), dielectric constant, magnetic susceptibility.
5. Thermal properties-Thermal conductivity, heat of reactions, transition temperature.
6. Nuclear properties-Radio activity, isotopic mass, etc.

3.1 Advantages of Instrumental Methods

1. Time saving.
2. Large number of samples can be handled at a time.
3. Variety of methods available. Hence, we can choose alternate methods.
4. Instruments have higher sensitivity and there is minimum personal error.
5. Wider applicability – solids as well as liquids can be determined.

3.2 Classification of Instrumental Methods

Electrometric methods	Electrolysis, Conductometry, Potentiometry, Polarography, Amperometry, Coulometry.
Optical methods	Colorimetry, Turbidimetry, Spectrophotometry, Flame Photometry, Spectrography, Polarimetry, X ray emission, Refrectometry
Thermal methods	Differential Thermal Analysis
Gas, Volumetric methods	Adsorption, Combustion

3.3 Conductometry

Solutions of electrolytes conduct an electric current by the migration of positively charged species towards the cathode and negatively charged anions towards the anode under the influence of an electric field. Solution of strong acids, strong bases and most salts are good conductors of electric current and obeys Ohm's law.

The resistance (R) is expressed in Ohms and the conductance of the solution is the reciprocal of its resistance and is expressed as 1/Ohms or mhos. Specific conductance is the conductance given by the solution between electrodes of 1 cm^2 and 1 cm apart.

Equivalent conductance is the conductance of a solution containing one gram equivalent weight of dissolved electrolyte between electrodes 1 cm apart. As solutions become dilute, their equivalent conductance increases.

Equivalent conductance = (1000 x specific conductance)/Normality

According to Ohm's law for the same type of material, the resistance is proportional to the length of the conductor and inversely to the cross section or diameter. The resistance offered decreases with electrolyte concentration in the solution and hence, the intensity of current flowing through the solution is directly proportional to the electrolyte concentration.

In conductivity measurements, the intensity of current flowing between two electrodes of known and constant surface area through the electrolyte solution is measured, keeping the distances between the electrodes constant.

A Conductometric titration involves the measurement of the conductance of the sample after successive addition of the reagent. The end point is determined from a plot of either the conductance or the specific conductance as a function of the volume of added titrant.

3.4 Potentiometry

Potentiometric titrations make practical use of the relationship between the concentrations of the components of the cell and the emf of a voltaic cell. That is near the end point, there is a sudden change in the emf or pH.

Potentiometric methods are highly useful in titrations involving turbid of highly coloured solutions where the use of chemical indicators is either unsatisfactory or impossible.

In Potentiometric titrations, the pH values of solutions are experimentally determined during the progress of titration. By plotting these values against corresponding volumes of titrating solutions added, curves with characteristic patterns are obtained. From these curves, the equivalence points can be obtained by finding the mid point of the inflection of the curve or by finding the point of maximum slope of the curve.

Potentiometric measurement is based on the Helmoltz electrode potential and Nernst equation as follows:

$E = (RT/ nF) \times 2.303 \text{ pH}$

$E = 0.058 \times \text{pH}$

$\therefore \text{pH} = E$, Since 0.058 is negligible

The potential difference is measured electronically by immersing a glass electrode with standard KCl-Calomel reference electrode. The potential measured in millivolts is recalibrated into pH units using the following formula of pH = (E – 0.246)/0.058.

3.5 Colorimetry

Colorimetry is quantitative analysis in which the quantity of a coloured constituent is determined by measuring the relative amount of absorption of light passing through a solution of the constituent.

Comparison is made directly or indirectly, by either visual or electrical means, between the intensity of light passing through the solution and the intensity of light of the same wave length passing through a solution (or series of solutions) of the same substance at known concentrations.

Colouring of the substances is of three types as follows:

1. The constituent itself may be coloured. e.g. determination of $KMnO_4$ ion.
2. The constituent may be made to react with a substance to form a coloured compound. e.g. estimation of P in soils.
3. The constituent may be made to displace an equilibrium existing between two coloured compounds and thus give a definite, determinable intermediate shade of colour to the solution. e.g determination of pH of a solution from the colour produced by addition of an indicator.

Colorimetric methods are generally limited to determinations at relatively low concentration (< 2 %).

To understand Colorimetry, it is better to have a basic knowledge of light and its properties.

Light passes in the form of electromagnetic radiation. It is a form of energy transmitted at an enormous velocity. It is transmitted as waves having electric and magnetic components. The visible (light) range occupies only a small region in the spectrum of electromagnetic radiations.

Wave length is the distance between two maxima of an electromagnetic wave. It is expressed as meters, centimeters, millimeters, micron (m) (1 in million), milimicron (mm), nanometer (nm) and Angstrom (A°) units.

1 A° = 10^{-8} cm = 10^{-7} mm = 10^{-10} m = 0.1 nm

1 nm = 1 mm = 10^{-9} m = 10^{-7} cm = 10^{-6} mm = 10 A°

The major components of electromagnetic spectrum are as follows:

Gamma ray region	0.02 – 1 A° (shortest waves emitted by atomic nuclei)
X ray region	1 – 10 A°(emitted due to movement of electron close to the nuclei of heavy atoms)
Ultraviolet region	
Vacuum ultraviolet	1 – 180 nm
Ultraviolet	180 – 400 nm
Visible region	(400 – 750 nm)
Violet	400 – 435 nm
Blue	435 – 480 nm
Green Blue	480 – 490 nm
Blue green	490 – 500 nm
Green	500 – 560 nm
Yellow Green	560 – 580 nm
Yellow	580 – 595 nm
Orange	595 – 610 nm
Red	610 – 750 nm
Infra red region	
Near infra red	0.7 – 2.5 m
Infra red	2.5 – 15.0 m
Far infra red	15 – 200 m
Microwave region	0.1 mm – 1 cm
Radio frequency region	1 cm – 10 m

The energy of electromagnetic radiations is inversely related to the wave length. The energy of these electromagnetic radiations decreases from gamma to radio frequency waves.

Colorimetry is the determination of the concentration of a substance by measurement of the relative absorption of light or transmittance with respect to a known concentration of the substance. It is mainly based on Lambert's and Beer's Law.

According to Lambert's law, when a monochromatic light passes through an absorbing medium, its intensity decreases exponentially as the length / thickness of the medium increases.

According to Beer's law, the intensity of ray of monochromatic light passing through an absorbing medium decreases exponentially as the concentration of the absorbing medium increases.

Mathematically,

Lambert's law $T = (I / I_0) = 10^{-KL} = \log_{10} (I_0 / I) = K^1L$

Beer's law $T = (I / I_0) = 10^{-KC} = \log_{10} (I_0 / I) = K^1C$

Lambert's & Beer's law $T = (I / I_0) = 10^{-KCL} = \log_{10} (I_0 / I) = KCL$

Where,

I_0 = Intensity of incident light

I = Intensity of transmitted light (light leaving the solution)

K = Constant

L = Length of the absorbing medium

C = Concentration of the solution

T = Transmittance

From the above,

Absorbance (A) = $\mathrm{Log}_{10}(1/T)$

Where, T = Transmittance

The essential components of a colorimeter are as follows:

1. A source of radiant energy.
2. Some type of filter for isolation of a band of radiant energy.
3. An optical system for producing a parallel beam of filtered light for passage through an absorbing cell.
4. A detector.
5. Associated read out meters.

In the Colorimeter, the light converted into monochromatic by passing through a filter is passed through water / blank solution and the instrument is adjusted to

100% transmittance or zero optical density / absorbance. Then the solution containing the colour producing substance (chromogen) at various concentrations is placed in turn in the light path. Absorbance can also be calculated from the observed transmittance by using the following formula.

Absorbance = 2 – $\log_{10}$ (Transmittance)

From the optical density or transmittance is measured from the scale, a standard graph is prepared. Then the solution with the unknown concentration is placed and the optical density or transmittance is read from the scale. By referring to the standard graph, the actual concentration is determined.

3.6 Spectroscopy

Spectroscopy is the study of the spectral properties. The spectrum of light into the colours of which it is made is known as dispersion and the band produced by the dispersion is called as visible spectrum.

Generally, prisms or gratings are used to split the white light into seven colours as we seen in rainbows. Spectrophotometer is used to measure the intensity of specific spectral line of the light.

Instruments used to measure the intensity of spectra are as follows:

Colorimeter	Natural or artificial white light is generally used as a light source.
	It mainly uses a filter to isolate the wave length.
	A photocell or photo tube is used as a detector.
	It is used to measure absorption in the visible range.
Spectrophotometer	Light of definite wavelength, 1-10 A° band width, extending to the ultraviolet region of the spectrum constitutes the source of light.
	Monochromation is by prism or grating. Hence, the resolution of wave length is high.
	Photo tube or photo multiplier scatters to a wide range of wave length during estimation.
	It is used to measure the intensity of specific spectral line of the light.
Photometer	Used to measure the energy of transmitted light.
	It is a via media between Colorimeter and Spectrophotometer.

Spectroscopy is of three types as follows

- Flame Emission Spectroscopy (FES) / Flame Photometry
- Atomic Absorption Spectrophotometry (AAS)
- Emission Spectroscopy (ES)

3.7 Flame Photometry/ Flame Emission Spectroscopy

Flame Photometry is the study of the photon (light) energy emitted when a metal is introduced into the flame. It involves the measurement of the intensity of radiation emitted by the atoms that are excited by the high temperature of the flame. It is an important tool for the determination of alkali and alkaline earth metals for which the chemical methods are time consuming.

The elements present in the sample, when excited by the flame, emit photons of characteristic wave length and the intensity of which is related to the concentration of the element concerned.

Intensity of radiation α No of atoms in the sample

Fraction of atoms excited depends critically on the flame temperature. Hence, temperature control of the flame is very important in Flame Photometry. The important parts of Flame Photometer are as follows:

- Pressure regulator and flow meters for the fuel gases
- Atomizer
- Burner
- Optical system
- Photosensitive detector
- Instrument for recording the output of the detector

For Flame Photometry, the sample to be detected is prepared in solution form and sprayed under controlled conditions into a flame. The radiation from the flames enters a dispersing device to isolate the desired region of the spectrum. A phototube and some sort of meter or electronic amplifier measures the intensity of isolated radiation.

Before initiating the experiment, the Flame Photometer needs to be calibrated (preparation of a standard graph by employing different concentrations of a solution containing the element to be determined). Flame Photometers are generally employed for the estimation of sodium (Na) and potassium (K).

Radiation in the visible and ultra violet regions occurs when the atoms or molecules are excited by the absorption of energy. Each element has its own characteristic atomic spectrum which is very important in Flame Photometry.

The atomic spectrum of an element results when sufficient energy is supplied to volatilize the element and cause the electrons in the atoms or ions to move to higher energy status. The species is then said to be excited. The duration in the excited stage is very short (10^{-8} seconds).

The electrons tend to return spontaneously to their low energy levels frequently in series of discrete steps. Each of these steps involves the loss of definite amount of energy in the form of electromagnetic radiation. The wave length of this is determined by the magnitude of the energy difference between levels. As such, there are many possible excited states and multiplicity paths by which return to ground state can occur. Hence, many radiations of different wave lengths are produced by a given element. The collection of radiations for a given species, called emission spectrum is characteristic for that species alone.

Several methods are available for exciting the elements for analysis. One of the methods is heating the sample in a flame and cause excitation. In a Flame Photometer, emission fro excites atoms constitute the radiation source.

3.8 Atomic Absorption Spectrophotometry (AAS)

This method is especially useful for the determination of elements that are vaporized but not appreciably excited in oxyacetylene flame. The element of interest in the analysis is made the source of radiant energy and is subjected to electrical excitation causing to emit radiation of its characteristic frequencies. When this beam of light is passed the vaporized sample interposed between the source and the entrance slit of a monochromator, the atoms of the sample absorb this light and thus decrease the radiant power of the beam.

The radiant power of the spectral line is measured with a photomultiplier tube and amplifier, first without and then with sample on the optical beam. The decrease in radiant power is proportional to the number of atoms of the element of interest. e.g. estimation of micronutrients.

3.9 Chromatography

It is a process in which the species of interest are separated by differential migration in a porous medium, the migration being caused by the flow of some mobile phase. Thus the system consists of two phase *viz.,* one mobile/moving phase and another stationary phase, both being immersible with each other. There are different types of chromatography as follows:

Adsorption Chromatography (AC)	High Precision Liquid Chromatography (HPLC)
Thin Layer Chromatography (TLC)	Partition Chromatography
Gas Chromatography (GC)	Molecular sieve and Gel Permeation Chromatography
Gas – Liquid Chromatography (GLC)	Recycling Column Chromatography
Gas – Solid Chromatography (GSC)	Ion exchange Chromatography

4

Analytical Chemistry - Basic Calculations

Practice to calculate the weight / volume of reagents required to prepare the following standard solutions.

Preparation of Standard Solution - (1 *M*, 0.1 *M*, 1 *N*, 0.1 *N*, 0.5 *N*, 5%, 10%, 20%, 10 ppm, 20 ppm, 100 ppm)

1. Na_2CO_3
2. $NaHCO_3$
3. KCl
4. $KMnO_4$
5. KOH
6. $Fe_2SO_4.7H_2O$
7. $CaCl_2$
8. $MgCl_2$
9. NH_4OH
10. NaOH
11. $AgCl_2$
12. $CuSO_4$
13. HCl
14. HNO_3
15. H_2SO_4
16. CH_3COOH
17. H_3PO_4
18. $Ca(OH)_2$
19. KH_2PO_4
20. $KH(C_8H_4O_4)$

21. $K_2Cr_2O_7$
22. $MgSO_4$
23. $[K_3Fe(CN)_6]$
24. $[(C_6H_5)_2NH]$
25. $AgNO_3$
26. $Na_2S_2O_3$
27. $Fe_2SO_4\ (NH_4)_2SO_4.7H_2O$
28. NH_4Cl
29. $NaCl$
30. KNO_3

5

Analytical Chemistry - Basic Techniques

5.1 Volumetric Techniques or Titrimetric Analysis

1. Acid Base Neutralization Reactions-Acidimetry & Alkalimetry
2. Oxidation –Reduction Reactions-Oxidometry (Permanganometry) & Dichrometry
3. Precipitation Reactions-Thiocyanometry & Complexometry $V_1N_1 = V_2N_2$ (Law of Volumetric Analysis)

It is the analysis wherein determining the concentration of unknown solution using the given solution of known concentration.

5.2 Important Primary Standards

5.2.1 Acids

- Potassium Hydrogen Phthalate
- Benzoic Acid
- Constant boiling Hydrochloric Acid
- Sulphuric Acid
- Potassium Acid Iodate

5.2.2 Bases

- Sodium Carbonate
- Mercuric Oxide
- Borax

5.2.3 Oxidising Agents

- Potassium Dichromate
- Potassium Bromate
- Potassium Iodate

5.2.4 Reducing Agents

- Sodium Oxalate
- Arsenious Oxide
- Pure Iron Metal
- Potassium Ferro Cyanide

5.2.5 Others

- Sodium Chloride
- Potassium Chloride

5.3 Iodometry

It is the process in which standard solution of iodine is used. By determining its amount, the equivalent quantity of another element / radical is deduced. This process may be used to determine Sulphurous Acid, Sulphites, Sulphurated Hydrogen, Thiosulphate, Arsenite and Stannous Chloride. A 1% starch solution is used as indicator which gives an intense blue colour even with a very small amount of iodine.

5.4 Argentometry (Silver Nitrate titrations)

The metallic halides like chlorides, bromides and iodides can be estimated by titrating them in a solution against standard Silver Nitrate solution.

5.5 Gravimetric analysis

In this analysis, the substance to be estimated is separated from the rest of the sample as an insoluble compound or precipitate of known chemical composition and the final measurement is made by weighing. The precipitate is often ignited before weighing to convert into a substance of a definite chemical composition and of adequate chemical stability.

e.g. Estimation of Sulphate

6

Preparation of Primary Standard Solutions

Principle

Standard solutions are the solutions of accurately known concentrations. There are two types of standard solutions viz., primary and secondary.

A known quantity of the substances is dissolved in a volumetric flask and the volume is made upto the mark. Standard solutions prepared in this way are known as primary standard. This method can be used for preparation of standard solutions of substances which satisfy the following conditions.

- The substances must be chemically pure *i.e.* it must not contain impurities in amounts which could affect analytical precision (not more than 0.05 to 0.1 %). In other words, the substances must be of known and high degree of purity.
- The substances must be stable on keeping both in the solid state and in the solution, as otherwise its composition would cease to its formula.
- It must be non hygroscopic and not easily affected by acid fumes, CO_2 etc., inside the laboratory.
- The gram equivalent of the substance should be as large as possible, so that the precision in determining the normality of the solution in high.
- The substance must withstand fairly high temperature, so that it can be dried at 100° C.
- The substance must be freely soluble in water.
- The substance must be preferably solid and crystalline compounds.

Chemicals that can be chosen as primary standards

1. Succinic acid
2. Oxalic acid
3. Potassium Hydrogen Phthalate
4. Benzoic acid

5. Sulfamic acid
6. Sodium Carbonate
7. Borax
8. Sodium Oxalate
9. Potassium Dichromate
10. Arsenic trioxide
11. Sodium Chloride

Example: Preparation of 0.1 *N* Na_2CO_3 of 250 mL

Molecular weight of Na_2CO_3	=	106
Valency	=	2
Equivalent weight of Na_2CO_3	=	Molecular weight/ Valency
Therefore, one gram equivalent weight of Na_2CO_3	=	106 / 2 = 53

53 g dissolved in 1 litre gives 1 *N* solution

∴ " 5.3 g dissolved in 1 litre gives 0.1 *N* solution

∴ " 1.325 g dissolved in 250 mL gives 0.1 *N* solution of Na_2CO_3

Reagents Required

1. Analar Grade Na_2CO_3

Apparatus Required

1. 250 mL volumetric flask with stopper
2. Funnel
3. Chemical balance with weight box or Electronic balance

Procedure

- Weigh 1.325 g of sodium carbonate (AR Grade, oven dried at 110° C).
- Transfer this into a 250 mL volumetric flask using a funnel.
- Wash the funnel, collecting the washings in the flask.
- Remove the funnel and add about 100 mL of distilled water to the flask.
- Shake the flask thoroughly well so as to dissolve Na_2CO_3.
- Add if necessary, one more installment of 100 mL of water and again shake and thoroughly mix the contents ensuring complete dissolution of Na_2CO_3.

- Make up the volume to 250 mL and again shake so as to make uniform solution.
- Label the solution and preserve for the future use.
- The label must consist of name of the chemical, strength, date of preparation and name of the person who prepared the solution.

7

Preparation of Secondary Standard Solution of an Acid

More often, if the reagent is not a primary standard, a secondary standard solution must be prepared. The chemical is dissolved and made up or diluted to the desired concentration and then it is standardized against a primary standard or against another reliably known secondary standard solution. Such solutions are called as secondary standard solutions.

Principle

Equal volumes of all acids / bases containing their gram equivalent weights per litre of the solution react completely with each other.

$Na_2CO_3 + 2\ HCl \rightarrow 2\ NaCl + H_2O + CO_2$

$Na_2CO_3 + 2\ HNO_3 \rightarrow 2\ NaNO_3 + H_2O + CO_2$

$Na_2CO_3 + H_2SO_4 \rightarrow Na_2SO_4 + H_2O + CO_2$

In other words, the product of volume (V_1) and normality (N_1) of one solution (Acid) is equal to the product of volume (V_2) and normality (N_2) of another solution (Alkali/ Base).

From this it is clear that, **$V_1N_1 = V_2N_2$ (Law of Volumetric Analysis)**

Example: Preparation of 0.1 *N* HCl of 250 mL

Molecular weight of HCl	= 36.45
Valency	= 1
Equivalent weight of HCl	= Molecular weight / Valency
Therefore one gram equivalent weight of Na_2CO_3	= 36.45/1 = 36.45 g
Specific gravity of concentrated HCl	= 1.18 g / mL
Percent purity of concentrated HCl	= 35 %
One liter of 1 *N* solution of HCl contains	= 36.45 g of HCl
One liter of 0.1 *N* solution of HCl contains	= 3.645 g of HCl
To calculate the volume of conc. HCl that contains this amount of HCl	

By proportion for 35 g of HCl, 100 g of HCl is required Therefore for 3.645 g of HCl	=	(100 / 35) x 3.645 = 10.4 g of HCl
To convert this weight of HCl to volume basis, it must be divided by the specific gravity of the acid (1.18), We then have	=	10.4 / 1.18 = 8.8 mL of HCl
So, to prepare 1 litre of solution of 0.1 *N* HCl 8.8 mL of HCl is required Then for 250 ml of 0.1 *N* HCl	=	(8.8 / 1000) x 250 = 2.2 mL
Therefore, 2.2 mL of HCl is required to prepare 250 mL of 0.1 *N* HCl solution		

Reagents Required

1. Concentrated HCL
2. 0.1 *N* Na_2CO_3
3. Methyl orange indicator

Apparatus Required

1. 400 mL Beaker
2. 10 mL Measuring cylinder
3. 50 mL Burette
4. 10 mL Pipette
5. 250 mL Conical flask
6. 250 mL Measuring cylinder
7. Glass rod

Procedure

- Measure out 250 ml of distilled water into a 400 mL beaker using a 250 mL measuring cylinder.
- Add 2.2 mL (approximately 2.5 mL) of concentrated HCl through a 10 mL measuring cylinder to the beaker containing water.
- Thoroughly mix it using a glass rod. This is approximately a 0.1 *N* HCl solution.
- Now, fill up a burette with 0.1 *N* Na_2CO_3 (primary standard) and mount it in a burette stand.
- Pipette out 10 mL of the approximately 0.1 *N* solution of HCl into a 250 mL conical flask and add a few drops of methyl orange indicator. Note down the initial reading of the burette.

- Titrate the contents of conical flask against 0.1 *N* Na_2CO_3. End point is the change of colour from red to pale yellow.
- Tabulate the burette readings and find out the volume of 0.1 *N* Na_2CO_3 used in the titration.
- Repeat the titration until getting concordant titre values.
- Now using the relationship of law of volumetric analysis $V_1N_1 = V_2N_2$, find out the normality of the HCl.
- If the Na_2CO_3 consumed is exactly 10 mL then according to the above relationship, the normality of the prepared HCl solution is 0.1 *N*.
- If not, the normality of the prepared HCl solution may be higher or lower than 0.1 *N*.

Calculation

Volume of Na_2CO_3 consumed in the titration (V_1)	=	X mL
Volume of 0.1 *N* HCL taken (V_2)	=	10 mL
Normality of Na_2CO_3 (N_1)	=	0.1 *N*
Normality of the HCl prepared (N_2)	=	Y *(N)*
We know that, **$V_1N_1 = V_2N_2$ (Law of Volumetric Analysis)**		
X x 0.1	=	10 x Y
N_2 = Y	=	(X x 0.1) / 10

- Calculate the volume of water to be added in case of the normality is more than 0.1 *N* or the volume of concentrated HCl to be added in case the normality is less than 0.1 *N*.

If the prepared solution is more than 0.1 N

Volume of 0. 1 *N* HCl taken (V_2)	=	10 mL
Volume of 0.1 *N* Na_2CO_3 used in the titration (V_1)	=	X mL
Amount of water to be added for 10 mL of HCl	=	X – 10 mL
Therefore, the amount of water to be added for (250-A) mL of HCl solution	=	[(X – 10) / 10] x (250 –A) mL

Where, A = Volume of the prepared HCl solution already used for rinsing the pipette and or for titration

If the prepared solution is less than 0.1 N

Volume of 0. 1 *N* HCl taken (V_2)	=	10 mL
Volume of 0.1 *N* Na_2CO_3 used in the titration (V_1)	=	X mL
Normality of Na_2CO_3 (N_1)	=	0.1 *N*
We know that, $\mathbf{V_1N_1 = V_2N_2}$ **(Law of Volumetric Analysis)**		
$N_2 = Y$	=	V_1N_1 / V_2
$N_1 - N_2 = 0.1 - Y = z\,(N)$		
For the present 250 mL of 0.1 *N* HCl, we have taken 2.5 mL of conc. HCl		
Therefore for z (N) = [(2.5 XY) / 0.1] x (250 – A) / 250 mL		

- Add either the volume of water or the volume of acid as the case may be to the solution prepared in 400 mL beaker and mix it thoroughly by stirring.
- Repeat the titration and calculation processes until the normality of the HCl prepared attains 0.1 *N*.

Format of Titration Table

0.1 *N* Na_2CO_3 Vs Approximately 0.1 *N* HCl

S. No.	Aliquot taken in the pipette (mL)	Burette Readings (mL)		Volume of Titrant used (mL)	Indicator	End Point
		Initial	Final			

8

Preparation of Secondary Standard Solution of a Base

Principle

Equal volumes of all acids / bases containing their gram equivalent weights per litre of the solution react completely with each other.

$2\ KOH + 2\ HCl \rightarrow 2\ KCl + 2H_2O$

In other words, the product of volume (V_1) and Normality (N_1) of one solution (Acid) is equal to the product of volume (V_2) and Normality (N_2) of another solution (Alkali/ Base).

$V_1N_1 = V_2N_2$ (Law of chemical equivalent / Law of volumetric analysis)

Example: Preparation of 0.1 N HCl of 250 mL

Molecular weight of KOH	=	56
Valency	=	1
Equivalent weight of KOH	=	56 / 1 = 56
One gram equivalent weight of KOH	=	56 g
56 g dissolved in 1 litre gives 1 *N* of KOH solution		
∴ 5.6 g dissolved in 1 litre gives 0.1 *N* solution		
∴ 1.4 g dissolved in 250 mL of 0.1 *N* solution		

Procedure

- Weigh 1.4 g of KOH and transfer this to a 400 mL beaker and add 100 mL of distilled water and dissolve it by stirring with a glass rod.
- Add the remaining 150 mL of water to the beaker. This is approximately 0.1 *N* solution of KOH.
- Now, fill up burette with 0.1 *N* HCl (secondary standard) and mount it in the burette stand.
- Pipette out 10 mL of the approximately 0.1 *N* KOH into a 250 mL conical flask and add few drops of phenolphthalein indicator. Then the colour of the solution will become pink.

- Titrate against 0.1 *N* HCl upto an end point of disappearance of pink colour.
- Note down the burette readings and find out the volume of 0.1 *N* HCl used in the titration.
- Repeat the titration until getting concordant titre values.
- Now, using the relationship, $V_1N_1 = V_2N_2$, find out the normality of the KOH solution prepared.
- Calculate the volume of water to be added in case of the normality is more than 0.1 *N* or the amount of KOH to be added in case the normality is less than 0.1 *N*.
- Add either the volume of water or the amount of KOH, as the case may be and mix it thoroughly by stirring.
- Repeat the titration and calculation processes until the normality of the KOH prepared reaches 0.1 *N*.

Format of Titration Table

0.1 *N* HCl Vs Approximately 0.1 *N* KOH

S.No.	Aliquot takenin the pipette (mL)	Burette Readings (mL)		Volume of Titrant used (mL)	Indicator	End Point
		Initial	Final			

9

Collection and Preparation of Soil Samples for Laboratory Analysis

Soil is analyzed to know the nature of soil, to classify and advocate to farmers about the peculiarities of the soils and how much of fertilizers should be applied for better crop production.

A composite soil, of course, can not be moved to into a laboratory. The value of the laboratory work depends upon care in sampling. Each soil sample needs to be a fair representative of the specific area or horizon worth sampling.

If the sample is to be a representative of an area, it is necessary to take large number of samples spread over the area, pool them and sub-sample it so as to get a sample of desired size. For soil survey work, samples are collected from a profile which is typical of the soil of the surrounding area.

Materials Required

1. Spade
2. Khurpi
3. Auger (Screw or posthole type)
4. Core sampler
5. Soil testing tube (for wet soil)
6. Sampling bags and
7. Plastic basin or Bucket

Collection of soil samples from the field

- Normally each field may be treated as a sampling unit. But two or more fields, which are similar in appearance, production and past-management practices, may be grouped together into a single sampling unit.
- Samples should be collected separately from areas, which differ in soil colour or past-management practices such as liming, fertilization, cropping pattern etc.

- During the collection of soil, avoid dead furrows, old manure or lime piles, wet spots, areas near trees, manure pits, compost pits and irrigation channels.
- The sampling should be done in a zig zag pattern across the field to get homogeneity.
- A wise soil sample collecting agent is one who collects samples in the presence of the owner or cultivator of the land who is the best judge in deciding which area of his farm should be sampled separately.
- Scrap away the surface litter and insert the sampling auger to plough depth (15 cm).
- Take at least 15 samples randomly distributed over each area and place them in a clean bucket.
- If a sampling auger is not available, make a 'V' shaped cut to a depth of 15 cm using a mamutty or spade and remove 1.0 to 1.5 cm thick slice of soil from top to bottom of exposed face of the 'V' shaped cut and place them in a clean bucket.
- Thoroughly mix the samples taken from 15 or more spots of each area.
- Remove foreign bodies such as plant roots, stubbles, pebbles, stones or gravels.
- By Quartering, discard all but 0.5 to 1 kg of soil.
- Quartering is done by dividing the thoroughly mixed soil into four equal parts and discarding two opposite quarters.
- Remix the remaining two quarters and again divide into four equal parts and reject the opposite two.
- Repeat this procedure until to get 0.5 to 1 kg of soil.
- Instead of quartering, compartmentalization method can also be followed.
- For this, spread the soil on a clean hard surface and mark lines from both sides and create number of compartments.
- Take a little quantity of soil from each compartment and put into a clean container.
- Repeat the process of collection until the required quantity of soil is collected.
- Store the soil in a clean bag or container with proper labelling for further analysis.
- Sampling should be done after the harvest of the crop.

- In case the sampling is necessary during crop growth, sample between lines of growing plants.
- Avoid storing samples in fertilizer bags.

Collection of soil samples from a profile

- After the profile has been exposed, clean one face of the pit carefully with a spade and note the succession and depth of each horizon.
- Prick the surface with a knife or edge of the spade to show up the structure, colour and compactness of soil.
- Describe the profile as per the standard terminologies.
- Use Munsell colour chart for noting the colour and find out the texture by feel method.
- Collect the samples from each horizon by holding a large basin at the bottom limit of the horizon while the soil above is loosened by a khurpi.
- The sample is mixed and transferred to a bag after labelling.

Preparation of Soil Samples for Analysis

- The soil samples received at the laboratory should be air dried in shade and spread on a sheet of paper after breaking large lumps if present, with a wooden mallet.
- It is further ground by pounding with a wooden mallet in such a way that the aggregate particles are broken down to ultimate soil particles.
- The soil thus prepared is sieved through a sieve with round holes of 2 mm in diameter.
- The material on the sieve is again ground and sieved till all aggregate particles are fine enough to pass through and only stones and organic residues remain on the sieve.
- Mix well the 'fine soil' got by sieving and store in a suitable bottle or container with one label on the outside and another inside the container.
- For determination of organic carbon, powder and sieve the soil through 0.2 mm sieve.
- From the soil samples meant for micronutrient analysis, iron, brass, copper and zinc containers must be avoided for collection and storage of soil samples.

Sub-sampling for analysis

- The soil in the bottle is emptied on a clean thick sheet of paper and evenly spread with a sampling knife.

- It is heaped into a cone by raising the four ends of the paper.
- It is again mixed well and evenly spread on the paper as before.
- The process is repeated 3 to 4 times to ensure uniformity and then finally spread evenly on the paper again.
- Now it is divided into four quarters and small quantity of soil is taken for various points in each quarter to get a representative sample for analysis.

10

Determination of Soil Moisture

Principle

Soil moisture content is determined by drying a known quantity of soil sample in an electric oven at 105° C to 110° C and finding out the loss in weight.

Materials Required

1. Moisture bottle / Aluminum box
2. Chemical balance / Top pan balance
3. Desiccator

Procedure

- Place a clean and empty moisture bottle or aluminum box with lid separately in an electric oven and keep it at 105° C for 15 minutes.
- Replace the stopper or lid, remove the moisture bottle or aluminum box, cool in a desiccator.
- Weigh accurately and record the weight.
- Fill the moisture bottle or aluminum box to about two third of its capacity with soil sample.
- Close with stopper / lid and weigh quickly.
- Remove the stopper / lid and keep it in the oven at 105° C for about 8 hours.
- After expiry of time, remove the moisture bottle or aluminum box, cool it in a desiccator and weigh quickly.
- Calculate the loss in weight and express the moisture content on oven dry basis.

Calculation

Weigh of empty moisture bottle	=	A g
Weight of the moisture bottle + moist Soil sample	=	B g
Weight of moist Soil alone	=	(B-A) g
Weight of the moisture bottle + Soil Sample after drying	=	C g
Weight of moisture in the Soil	=	(B-C) g
Percentage of moisture in the Soil Sample on oven dry basis	=	[(B-C) / (C-A)] x 100

11

Determination of Bulk Density, Particle Density and Pore Space of Soil

(Cylinder Method)

Bulk density is the mass per unit volume of soil including pore space. The normal range of bulk density in most soils is ranging from 1.02 to 1.80 g / cm^3. The bulk density of coarse textured soils will be on the higher side while organic soils will have lower bulk density.

Particle density is the mass of soil per unit volume excluding pore space.

Pore space is that fraction of soil volume not occupied by solid particles.

Principle

The bulk density and percent pore space are determined from the apparent and true volumes of the soil measures by adding a known quantity of water to a measuring cylinder contain a weighed quantity of soil.

Materials Required

1. Measuring cylinder (100 mL) with glass stopper
2. Chemical balance or Electronic Balance

Procedure

- Weigh exactly 20g of soil sample and transfer in small quantities at a time to a 100 mL measuring cylinder with glass stopper by gently tapping the cylinder.
- After completely transferring the soil, note the volume.
- Add a known volume of water (50 mL) along the sides of the cylinder using pipette till the entire soil mass is completely soaked.
- There should be at least 5 mL of water above the soil surface after addition of water.

- Care should be taken to see that the final volume of soil and water is below 100 mL mark.
- Keep the cylinder with soil and water in an undisturbed condition for at least 30 minutes so that the entire pore space is completely filled with water.
- Note the final volume of soil plus water after the expiry of time and calculate the percentage the bulk density, particle density and percentage of pore space.

Calculation

Weigh of Soil taken	=	W (20) g
Volume of Soil taken	=	V_1 mL
Volume of Water added	=	V_2 mL
Volume of Soil + Water	=	$V_1 + V_2$ mL
Volume of the Soil Water at the end of the experiment	=	V_3 mL
Pore Space Volume	=	$[(V_1 + V_2) - V_3]$ mL
Percent Pore Space	=	$\{[(V_1 + V_2) - V_3] / V_1\} \times 100$
Bulk Density $[W/ V_1]$	=	$[W/ V_1]$ g / cm^3 or Mg / m^3
Particle Density	=	W / (V_1 – Pore Space volume)W / $(V_1 - [(V_1 + V_2) - V_3]$ g / cm^3 or Mg / m^3

12

Determination of Soil Texture

(International/Robinson's Pipette Method)

Principle

This method is based on Stoke's law. According to this law, the rate of fall of a particle in liquid is directly proportional to the square of its radius.

$V \alpha \ r^2$

$V = 2/9 \ g \ r^2 \ (dp\text{-}d) / \eta$

Where,

V = sedimentation velocity (cm/sec)

g = acceleration due to gravity (cm/sec^2)

r = radius of the particle or sphere (cm)

dp = Density of the particle (g/cc)

d = Density of the liquid (g/cc)

h = Viscosity of the liquid

The soil is first dispersed by destroying the binding agents with hydrogen peroxide and hydrochloric acid followed by treatment with a dispersing agent. Clay and silt are separated by sedimentation and coarse and fine sand by sieving.

Materials Required

1. 1000 mL spoutless Measuring cylinder
2. 500 mL Beaker
3. Rubber stopper for the cylinder
4. Mechanical stirrer
5. Funnel (7.5 cm diameter)
6. Filter paper - Whatman No.50
7. Filter stand

8. 150 mL Measuring cylinders
9. Water bath
10. Stop clock
11. Chemical balance
12. Tall form Beaker
13. Robinson Pipette
14. Hot air oven
15. Porcelain dish/basin
16. 6 % Hydrogen peroxide
17. *N*/5 Hydrochloric acid
18. Normal Sodium hydroxide

Procedure

- Transfer exactly 20 g air dried sample to a 500 mL beaker.
- Add 60 mL of 6 % hydrogen peroxide.
- Stir it well and keep it on a water bath for 30 minutes till frothing ceases.
- Treatment with hydrogen peroxide is to destroy the organic matter which is binding the soil particles.
- Hydrogen peroxide treatment is not necessary when the organic matter content of the soil is negligible.
- Then add 200 ml of *N*/5 HCl, stir well and keep it over night.
- Hydrochloric acid is added to destroy calcium carbonate present in the soil which is also acting as a binding agent.
- Filter the contents through Whatman No.50 filter paper and wash it with water till the filtrate runs free of chloride (collect about 10 mL of the filtrate in a test tube and add 2-3 drops of silver nitrate solution and formation of curdy white precipitate indicates the presence of chloride).
- When the filtrate runs free of chloride, transfer the soil material from the filter paper to another 500 mL beaker and add about 400 mL of water.
- Then add 8 mL of Normal sodium hydroxide and stir it well for 10 minutes with a mechanical stirrer.
- Transfer the contents to a 1000 mL spoutless measuring cylinder and make upto 1000 mL mark with water.

- Cover the cylinder tightly with a rubber stopper and shake the contents thoroughly by repeated inversions holding the rubber stopper tightly so as to avoid spilling of soil water suspension.

Clay and Silt

- Remove the rubber stopper and place the cylinder under Robinson pipette and start a stop clock simultaneously.
- Note down the temperature and settling time for clay plus silt from the table.
- Till the settling time is over, don't disturb the suspension.
- First lower the pipette in such a way that the tip of the pipette just touches the surface of the suspension.
- At the end of the stipulated settling time for clay plus silt, lower the pipette to 10 cm depth and draw 20 mL suspension and deliver it to a weighed clean porcelain dish. This suspension contains clay plus silt.
- Evaporate this first by keeping it on a water bath and dry it in hot air oven at 105°C.
- Cool it in a desiccator and determine the weight of clay plus silt and calculate the percent of clay plus silt.

Clay Alone

- Shake the contents of the cylinder well and allow undisturbed till the stipulated settling time for clay alone corresponding to the suspension temperature.
- Withdraw 20 mL of the suspension at the end of the period as done in the case of clay plus silt and determine the weight as clay alone after evaporating and drying.

Coarse Sand and Fine Sand

- Pour out major portion of the suspension from the cylinder after with drawing sample for clay alone.
- While pouring out care should be taken to see that no sand fraction is lost.
- Then wash the sediment with water and transfer the contents to a tall-form beaker.
- Add water to a height of more than 10 cm and stir well and allow it stand for 4 minutes.
- Then pour off the supernatant liquid and repeat this process till the water poured off is no longer turbid.

- Transfer the residue to a porcelain basin, dry it in hot air oven and weigh as coarse sand plus fine sand.
- Sieve the coarse sand and fine sand in a 70 mesh sieve. The material passing through the sieve will be the fine sand while the coarse sand fraction will be retained on the sieve.

Calculation

Clay + Silt

Weight of Soil taken	=	20 g
Volume of the suspension	=	1000 mL
Volume of the suspension pipetted out	=	20 mL
Weight of empty porcelain dish	=	A g
Weight of Silt + Clay + dish + NaOH	=	B g
Weight of Clay +Silt + NaOH		(B-A) g
Weight of NaOH Alone (present in 20 mL of suspension)	=	0.0064 g
Weight of Clay + Silt alone	=	B – (A + 0.0064) g = C
Percent Clay +Silt	=	C x (1000/20) x (100/20)

Clay Alone

Weight of empty porcelain dish	=	P g
Weight of dish + Clay + NaOH	=	Q g
Weight of Clay + NaOH	=	(Q –P) g
Weight of NaOH alone (present in 20 mL of suspension)	=	0.0064 g
Weight of Clay alone	=	Q – (P + 0.0064) g = R
Percent Clay	=	R x (1000/20) x (100/20)
Percent Silt	=	(Percent Clay +Silt) – Percent Clay

Coarse Sand + Fine Sand

Weight of Porcelain Basin	=	X g
Weight of dish + Coarse sand + Fine Sand	=	Y g
Weight of Coarse Sand + Fine Sand alone	=	(Y – X) g
Percent Coarse Sand + Fine Sand	=	(Y – X) x (100/20)

Coarse Sand Alone

Weight of Porcelain Basin	=	C g
Weight of dish + Coarse Sand	=	D g
Weight of Coarse Sand alone	=	(D – C) g
Percent Coarse Sand	=	(D – C).x (100/20)
Percent Fine Sand	=	[Percent Coarse Sand + fine Sand) - (Percent Coarse sand)]

Sedimentation time for clay and silt fractions

(Depth of sedimentation is 10 cm)

Temperature	Sedimentation time for clay		Sedimentation time for silt	
	Hrs	Min	Min	Sec
8	1	0	6	40
9	10	40	6	30
10	10	25	6	20
11	10	10	6	10
12	9	50	6	0
13	9	35	5	50
14	9	20	5	40
15	9	5	5	30
16	8	50	5	20
17	8	35	5	10
18	8	25	5	5
19	8	10	5	0
20	8	0	4	48
21	7	50	4	40
22	7	40	4	30
23	7	25	4	30
24	7	15	4	20
25	7	5	4	15
26	6	0	4	10
27	6	45	4	5
28	6	40	4	0
29	6	30	3	55
30	6	20	3	50
31	6	15	3	45
32	6	5	3	40
33	5	55	3	35

13

Determination of Infiltration Rate of Soil

Principle

When water is ponded inside the concentric metallic rings driven into the soil, the rate of recession (fall) of the water level, or the rate of water withdrawn from a supply source used to maintain a constant head of water on the soil surface, gives the infiltration rate of the soil.

During infiltration of water into the soil, appreciable lateral movement of water may also occur. To avoid the error due to this lateral movement, two concentric rings are used. Equal heights of water are to be maintained in both the rings. The infiltration is measured in the inner ring only. The rate of water intake per unit area varies markedly with the size of the rings and the depth of the soil to which they are driven into. Infiltration rate studies are preceded by the profile, initial soil moisture and any other problems of the region in which the soil is located.

Apparatus Required

1. Double ring infiltrometer: Cylinders made up of 14 to 16 gauge iron sheet, rolled in circular fashion and joints are ground to a smooth finish. One end of the cylinders is sharpened from outside keeping inside completely smooth. This facilitates easy drive of the cylinders into the soil. Diameter of the inner and outer cylinder is generally 30-35 cm and 40-45 cm respectively.
2. Circular driving caps or plates made up of iron with 1-1.5 cm thickness and 5-10 cm larger in diameter than the diameter of the largest cylinder.
3. Hammer of sufficient weight to drive the rings into the soil.
4. Hook gauge or staff gauge
5. Field source of water
6. Thermometer
7. Stop clock or Watch
8. Rubber or plastic sheet to be used as a splash guard

Procedure

- Select a representative area in the field.
- Examine for its texture, structure and water content.
- Record the conditions of soil surface such as surface litter or mulch, uncultivated with crust and or cracked surface or freshly cultivated with friable cloddy surface etc.
- Set the inner cylinder in the selected place and drive it vertically downwards into the soil with the help of driving plate and hammer to a desired depth (generally 10 – 20 cm depth).
- Care should be taken that the soil is disturbed to a minimum and cylinder is driven straight downward from all sides.
- Tap the soil into the space between the soil column and the inner side of the cylinder to its natural condition as far as practicable.
- Set the outer ring concentric to the inner one and drive it into the same depth taking the same precautions as taken in the case of inner ring.
- Cover the soil with a splash guard and apply 10- 15 cm water in the inner ring as well in the space between inner and outer ring almost simultaneously.
- Then remove the splash guard and measure the level of water in the inner cylinder with the gauge keeping edge of the cylinder as reference level.
- Record the recession of water in the inner cylinder at 1, 3, 5, 10, 30, 40, 60, 80, 100, 120 minutes and hourly thereafter till the water intake is almost constant. However, the time intervals of observation can be varied according to the objectives of the study and soil permeability. If all the ponded water soaks into the soil in a short period, more water may be ponded and the recession of water recorded again and again till the constant intake is reached.
- Record the water level and time just before and after reponding. Keep the interval between these two observations as short as possible to avoid errors caused by intake during the refilling period.
- Tabulate the observations in the following format and calculate the infiltration rate of the soil.

S. No.	Cumulative time (min)	Piezometer reading	Time interval	Infiltration rate (cm min^{-1})
1.				
2.				
3.				
4.				
5.				
6.				

Precautions

- Install infiltrometer straight in order to minimize the soil surface disturbance.
- Cover the soil surface in the rings with polythene sheet (splash guard) while pouring water in the rings.
- Try to keep water level identical in the inner and outer ring.
- If the evaporation rate is high during summer, cover the water surface with oil film to minimize the error due to evaporation.
- The temperature of the infiltration water should be same as that of soil to avoid soil air being dissolved in the infiltration water thus increasing infiltration rate. This happens when temperature of the water is more than the soil. Reverse will be the case if infiltration water is cooler than the soil.
- Water used in infiltrometer tests must be of same quality and composition as the water in the real system for which the infiltration rate is to be determined.

Calculation

Infiltration rate = $[(P_2 - P_1) / 2\ (T_2 - T_1)] \times 60$ cm hr^{-1}

Where, P_1 and P_2 are the initial and final Piezometer readings T_1 and T_2 are the initial and final time

Interpretation

Infiltration Rate (cm hr^{-1})	Rating
< 0.1	Very Slow
0.1 – 0.5	Slow
0.5 – 2.0	Moderately Slow
2.0 – 6.3	Moderate
6.3 – 12.7	Moderately Rapid
12.7 – 25.4	Rapid
> 25.4	Very Rapid

14

Determination of Maximum Water Holding Capacity of Soil

(Keen-Rackzowski/Hilgard Apparatus Method)

Principle

With the capillary rise of water, the soil immediately above a water table gets saturated. The height upto which the soil is saturated depends on the texture, structure and packing of the soil mass. The experimental technique discussed herein permits approximation of maximum water holding capacity while determining the amount of water held in the soil at the point of saturation.

Apparatus Required

1. Keen Box
2. Flat bottomed soaking tray
3. Spatula
4. Physical balance
5. Oven
6. Filter paper
7. 2 mm sieve

Procedure

- Clean and dry the dish of Keen box and weigh the box alone.
- Cut out a Whatman No.1 or 44 filter paper and place it at the bottom of the box.
- Weigh the Keen box and filter paper and record it.
- Pass the air dry soil through a 2 mm sieve and fill the box with repeated tapping (20–30 time) on the top of a wooden table to enable complete an uniform packing.

- Level off the surface with the help of spatula / sampling knife.
- Weigh the keen box + filter paper + air dry soil.
- Place the box in the soaking tray and gradually fill the tray with water from the side till the water level is about 1 cm above the base of the box.
- Cover the tray to prevent evaporation from soil surface and let it rest for 12 – 16 hours until the equilibrium is reached to enable complete saturation of soil with water. This is confirmed by a continuous and shinning film of water at the soil surface.
- Carefully remove the box from water and wipe the box dry from outside and weigh it quickly.
- Place the Keen box with soil in a hot air oven at 105°C, supporting it on a triangle so as to allow free access of air to the perforated bottom.
- After drying to a constant weight, cool it in a desiccator and weigh it.
- Calculate the water holding capacity of soil as a percentage of the oven dry soil.

Calculation

Weight of the Keen box + Filter Paper	=	A g
Weight of the Keen box + Saturated Soil	=	B g
Weight of the Keen box + Oven dry Soil	=	C g
Weight of the wet Filter paper	=	D g
Maximum water holding capacity	=	Weight of the maximum water absorbed by the soil / Over dry weight of the soil
Maximum water holding capacity (%)	=	{[B – (C+D)] / [C – A]} x 100

15

Estimation of Soil pH

The pH is defined as negative logarithm of hydrogen ion concentration or the log of the reciprocal of the hydrogen ion concentration (Sorenson, 1906).

Principle

A glass electrode in contact with hydrogen ions of the solution acquires an electric potential which depends on the concentration of hydrogen ions. This is measured potentiometrically against some reference electrode which is usually a calomel electrode. The potential difference between glass electrode and calomel electrode is expressed in pH units.

Two electrodes are used in the determination of pH. One is reference electrode which provides a standard voltage and is usually a saturated calomel electrode which has two layers of saturated solution of KCl and mixture of solid $HgCl_2$ and Hg. The outer tube is usually 5-15 cm long, 0.5-1 cm in diameter. The mixture of solid $HgCl_2$ + Hg paste is contained in an inner tube that is connected to the saturated KCl solution in the outer tube by means of small opening. The resistance developed by this type of electrode is 2000-3000 Ohms.

The outer electrode is glass electrode that consists of a tube enclosing a lead wire made up of Ag coated with AgCl. This wire is again enclosed in a wax insulation. To the tube at the bottom is attached a glass bulb made up of a special kind of glass which is sensitive to hydrogen ions. The thickness of the glass membrane varies from 0.03 to 0.1 mm and has a resistance of 50 to 500 mega Ohms.

When these electrodes are dipped in solution, the saturated solution of KCl comes out of reference through small holes and forms an invisible ionic bridge between electrodes through which current passes. The hydrogen ions are absorbed by glass electrode and depending upon the amount of hydrogen ions present in the solution, an electric potential develops between electrodes. This potential difference is measured in terms of pH units by suitable Galvanometer.

Materials Required

1. pH Meter
2. 100 mL Beakers
3. Glass rod
4. pH Buffer Solutions (pH 4.0, 7.0, 9.2)

Procedure

Standardization of pH Meter

- Switch on the pH meter and allow it warm for 10 minutes.
- Keep the pH selector switch on zero position.
- Set the temperature compensation control to the solution temperature.
- Adjust the zero adjustment knob so that the pointer in the meter reads exactly zero, when the electrodes are immersed in distilled water.
- Lift electrodes from distilled water and wipe it dry using filter paper / tissue paper and dip them in standard buffer solution of known pH (4.0, 7.0, 9.2).
- Change the function switch to particular pH range (0 – 7 or 7 – 14) and adjust the standardization knob till the pointer reads the correct pH value of the buffer solution. Do not disturb the zero knob adjustment.

pH Measurement

- Weigh 20 g air dry soil passed through 2 mm sieve and transfer to a clean 100 mL beaker.
- Add 50 mL of distilled water (1: 2.5 ratio of soil water suspension).
- Using glass rod, stir the content intermittently and allow it stand for 30 minutes.
- Wash the electrodes carefully with a jet of distilled water and wipe it dry with a piece of filter / tissue paper.
- Stir the soil suspension again just before taking the reading in the pH meter.
- Immerse the electrodes into the beaker containing soil water suspension and change the function to the particular pH range.
- Record the meter reading as pH units.

16

Estimation of Electrical Conductivity of Soil

The Electrical Conductivity (EC) of the soil is a measure of soluble salts present in the soil and is expressed as millimhos/cm or dSm^{-1}.

Principle

As the amount of the soluble salts in a solution increases, the electrical conductivity also increases. This electrical conductivity is measured in terms of resistance offered to the flow of current using a conductivity bridge.

It is known that solutions offer some resistance to the passage of current through them, depending upon the concentration of the soluble salts present. Hence, EC is measured in terms of electrical Resistance between parallel electrodes immersed in the soil water suspension.

In such a system, the solution between the electrodes becomes the electrical conductor to which the physical laws relating to resistance are applicable. The electrical resistance 'R' is directly proportional to the distance 'L' between the electrodes and inversely proportional to the cross sectional area 'A' of the conductor.

Hence, $R = L/A$ or $R = r \times L/A$

Where,

r = proportionality constant known as electrical conductivity

If $L = 1$ cm and $A = 1$ cm^2, then $R = r$

Where, r is called specific resistivity. Hence specific resistance is the resistance of a conductor of 1 cm in length and 1 cm^2 in cross sectional area.

Higher the salt content, higher the passage of current and lesser the resistance to the flow of the current. Hence, the reciprocal of specific resistivity is called as specific conductivity. Therefore, specific conductivity is defined as the conductivity of a solution enclosed in a cell whose electrodes are exactly with 1 cm distance and possess a surface area of 1 cm^2. The resistance is expressed as Ohms/cm and the electrical conductivity is expressed as mhos/cm as the electrical conductivity is the reciprocal of electrical resistance.

It is not possible to make a conductivity bridge having electrodes 1 cm^2 in area and place exactly 1 cm apart. Hence, the factor called the cell constant is determined for the given cell as a correction factor. Modern conductivity meter are calibrated to read directly the electrical conductivity / conductance with given cell.

Materials Required

1. Conductivity Bridge / EC Meter
2. 100 ml Beaker
3. Glass rod
4. 0.1 *N* KCl solution
5. Saturated $CaSO_4$ solution

Procedure

- Switch on the EC meter / Conductivity Bridge and allow it to stand for 10 minutes.
- Check the instrument with saturated calcium sulphate solution and 0.1 *N* KCl solutions having 2.2 dSm^{-1} and 1.41 dSm^{-1} respectively.
- Use the same soil water suspension used for the pH measurement for the determination of EC.
- Stir the contents and allow the soil to settle for 15 minutes.
- Wash the electrodes carefully and immerse them into soil suspension.
- Adjust the temperature correction and adjust the meter knob until the magic eye of the null indicator is at the widest in width.
- The readings on the scale at this position indicate the electrical conductivity.
- Multiply this value of EC by cell constant usually noted on the cell itself to get specific conductivity.

17

Estimation of Organic Carbon Content of Soil

[Titrimetric/ Walkley and Black (1934) Method]

Introduction

The role of soil organic matter, in relation to soil fertility and physical conditions, are widely recognized. The organic matter is the source of plant nutrients which are released inassimilable forms during microbial degradation. A major proportion of N (95 – 99 % of the total), P (33 – 67 % of the total) and S (75 % of the total) in soils occur in organic combinations, which mineralize to release the nutrients in inorganic forms to be used by plants. Nevertheless, it serves as a reservoir of plant nutrients, in promoting water storage, and in regulating microbial activity.

The organic matter content of a soil varies from 0.344 % in very sandy arid soils to more than 86 % in Peats and Mucks. Soil organic matter contains 5 % N, and 0.5 % each of P and S, thereby, having a N:P:S ratio of 10:1:1. The organic matter content of a soil is estimated by the amount of organic carbon (C) present, as this element represents, on an average, 52 – 58 % of the organic matter, and the C:N ratio is 10 – 15. In the sub-soil, the average organic carbon amount is 36 – 44 % (40 %), and the C:N ratio is < 8. In order to find out the amount of humified organic material, the organic carbon content is multiplied by 1.724, which represents the ratio between the humus and the organic carbon (100/58) and is known as the 'von Bemmlen factor'.

The organic matter content of soils is estimated from the organic carbon, determined by using the 'Titrimetric method / Walkley and Black method. The Titrimetric determination, also known as the 'wet-digestion method' involves a rapid titration procedure for the estimation of organic carbon content of soils.

Importance

- For ordinary routine work, rapid titration method is useful to determine indirectly the N status of soil.

- However, the organic carbon status can not be taken as a reliable of available N, because the C:N ratio of different soils varies widely.
- Phosphorus and sulphur status of a soil can also be ascertained to a certain extent from such determination.
- This method oxidizes a lower percentage of the total organic C in soils. However, it has been found that, if this method is modified, by applying external heat, immediately adding sulphuric acid to the sample, the oxidation of organic C is nearly complete and the degree of oxidation is more consistent than in regular method.
- In the regular method, only 77 % organic carbon gets oxidized. So, a correction factor should be used in calculating the percentage of organic C in the end.

Principle

Organic carbon present in the organic matter is oxidized by chromic acid in the presence of concentrated sulphuric acid. Potassium dichromate on reaction with H_2SO_4 provides nascent oxygen, which combines with carbon and forms CO_2. The H_2SO_4 enables easy digestion of organic matter by rendering heat of dilution. Only certain quantity of chromic acid is used for oxidation. The excess chromic acid left unused by the organic matter is determined by back titration with 0.5 *N* ferrous sulphate or ferrous ammonium sulphate using diphenylamine indicator.

Reactions

$$2\,K_2Cr_2O_7 + 8\,H_2SO_4 \rightarrow 2\,K_2SO_4 + 2\,Cr_2\,(SO_4)_3 + 8H_2O + 6\,(O)$$

$$3\,C + 6\,(O) \rightarrow 3CO_2$$

Apparatus & Materials Required

1. 500 mL Conical flask
2. Pipette
3. Burette
4. Measuring cylinder

Reagents Required

1. 1 *N* Potassium Dichromate ($K_2Cr_2O_7$)
2. Concentrated H_2SO_4
3. 0.5 *N* Ferrous Sulphate (FS) or Ferrous Ammonium Sulphate (FAS)

4. Phosphoric acid (Ortho Phosphoric acid - 85 %)
5. Diphenylamine indicator

Procedure

- Weigh exactly 0.5 g of soil (passed through 0.5 mm sieve) and transfer it to a 500 mL conical flask.
- Add 10 mL of 1 *N* $K_2Cr_2O_7$ and mix well by swirling the flask. Then add 20 mL of concentrated H_2SO_4 and mix by gentle rotation for one minute to ensure complete contact of the reagent with the soil.
- Run a blank simultaneously (without soil, others remaining same).
- Allow the contents to stand for 20-30 minutes. Keep the flask preferably on an asbestos sheet to avoid burning of table due to intense heat.
- Add 200 mL of distilled water to dilute the solution.
- Add 10 mL of orthophosphoric acid and add 1 mL of diphenylamine indicator.
- Titrate the solution with 0.5 *N* ferrous ammonium sulphate.
- The colour is dull green at the beginning and then shifts to a turbid blue as the titration proceeds. The end point is very sharp and shifts to a bright green colour.

Observation and Calculation

Weight of soil taken	=	0.5 g
Volume of 1 *N* $K_2Cr_2O_7$ used	=	10 mL
Volume of 0.5 *N* ferrous ammonium sulphate (FAS) used for blank titration	=	X mL
Volume of 0.5 *N* Ferrous ammonium sulphate (FAS) used for sample titration	=	Y mL
X mL of FAS reduces	=	10 mL of 1 *N* $K_2Cr_2O_7$
Therefore Y mL of FAS reduces	=	Y/X x 10 mL
Hence, actual quantity of 1 *N* $K_2Cr_2O_7$ used for oxidation of organic matter	=	10-(10 x Y/X) mL
1 mL of 1 *N* $K_2Cr_2O_7$	=	0.003 g of C
Therefore 10-(10 x Y/X) mL of 1 *N* $K_2Cr_2O_7$	=	[10-(10 x Y/X)] x 0.003 g of C
This is present in 0.5 g of soil		
Therefore in 100 g of soil (or) % of organic carbon (OC) in the soil (uncorrected)	=	[10-(10 x Y/X)] x 0.003 x (100/0.5)
% of organic carbon in the soil (corrected)	=	[10-(10 x Y/X)] x 0.003 x (100/0.5) x 1.3
Organic matter (surface soil)	=	OC x 1.724
Organic matter (sub-surface soil)	=	OC x 2.5

Interpretation (Fertility Rating)

Amount of OC (%)	Comments
< 0.5	Low
0.5 – 0.75	Medium
> 0.75	High

Things to Learn

1. Why are we adding orthophosphoric acid in organic carbon estimation?
2. What is the role of sulphuric acid in organic carbon estimation?
3. What is the status of organic C in Indian soils?
4. How will you derive the conversion factor of 1.724?
5. Why a correction factor of 1.3 is used in calculating the % of organic C in soil?

18

Determination of Available Nitrogen in Soil

[Alkaline Permanganate / Subbiah and Asija (1956) Method]

Introduction

Nitrogen (N) is found in the arable horizon of the soil, mostly in organic material. In the soil solution, organic N is gradually transformed into ammoniacal (NH_4^+), nitrite (NO_2^-) and nitrate (NO_3^-) nitrogen by microbial processes. Organic-N is, in itself, of very little use to plants, as it can not be absorbed as such. It is, therefore, necessary to estimate the different forms of mineralized or available N. The NO_3^--N and NO_2^--N together, hardly, exceed 1 % of the total N in normal soil.

The available N in soil refers to a fraction of the total N which is converted into forms accessible to the plants. This constitutes, on an average, only 0.5-2.5 % (rarely 5 %) of the total N in a soil at any given time. Nitrogen is, generally, absorbed by plants as NO_3^-, under oxidized environment (upland condition), and as NH_4^+, under reduced condition. NO_2^- is sometimes, detectable, but the amount is, generally, very small *vis-a-vis* NH_4^+ or NO_3^- and, hence does not warrant its determination. The sum total of NH_4^+ and NO_3^-- N is smaller than the total N, which becomes available to plants and the difference being attributed to the mineralization of the organic N, during the crop growth cycle.

Importance

- The chemical analysis of the soil for N is less precise when the requirement for this element needs to be forecast over a long period of time, as they vary not only with species, but with the phase of growth and season as well.
- Therefore, the chemical analysis for NH_4^+ and NO_3^- signifies the momentary status when the sample is taken (valid for 15 - 20 days), and measures must be taken instantaneously.
- Nevertheless, the analysis of the extractable N content of soils, using a given extractant method, in relation to the crop response study, provides a basis for finding out its soil critical level, in order to place soils into categories,

on the basis of N-fertility levels, which will rationalize the use-efficiency of N-fertilizer in soils, under a given climatic condition.

Principle

A given weight of soil is treated with excess of alkaline $KMnO_4$ and distilled. $KMnO_4$ is a mild oxidizing agent in an alkaline medium. The organic matter present in the soil is oxidized by the nascent oxygen, liberated by $KMnO_4$, in the presence of NaOH, and, thus, the ammonia released is distilled, and absorbed in a known volume of a standard acid, the excess of which is titrated with a standard alkali, using methyl red as the indicator. N estimated by this method is considered to be hydrolysable N or potentially available N.

Reactions

A. Distillation

$$2KMnO_4 + H_2O \xrightarrow{\text{alkaline medium}} 2MnO_2 + 2KOH + O^-$$

$$RCH.NH_2COOH + O^- \xrightarrow{\text{oxidative deamination}} R.CO.COOH + NH_3$$

$$NH_3 + H_2O \xrightarrow{\text{distillation}} NH_4OH$$

$$2NH_4OH + H_2SO_4 \xrightarrow{\text{absorption}} (NH_4)_2SO_4 + 2H_2O$$

B. Titration

$$H_2SO_4 + 2NaOH \longrightarrow Na_2SO_4 + 2H_2O$$

Apparatus & Materials Required

1. Kjeldahl distillation set
2. Measuring cylinder
3. Pipette
4. Burette
5. Conical flask
6. Heater or Burner

Reagents Required

1. 0.32 % $KMnO_4$ solution – Dissolve 3.2 g of $KMnO_4$ in distilled water, and make up the volume to 1 litre.
2. 2.5 % NaOH solution – Dissolve 25 g of NaOH pellets in distilled water, and make up the volume to 1 litre.

3. N/50 H_2SO_4
4. N/50 NaOH
5. Methyl Red indicator (0.15 %) – Dissolve 0.15 g of Methyl Red powder in alcohol and make up the volume to 100 mL.
6. Glass beads and Liquid Paraffin or Paraffin Wax

Procedure

- Place 20 g of soil in a distillation flask. Add 20 mL of water just to moist the soil (do not add excess water) and 1 mL of liquid paraffin or 1 g paraffin wax.
- Add few pieces of glass beads and100 mL of freshly prepared 0.32 % $KMnO_4$ solution to the soil in the distillation flask.
- Pipette out 25 mL of *N*/50 H_2SO_4 in a conical flask. Add 2-3 drops of methyl red indicator, and dip the end of the delivery tube into it.
- Pour 100 mL of 2.5 % NaOH solution into the flask and cork immediately.
- Distil the ammonia gas from the distillation flask and collect in H_2SO_4 solution. Continue the distillation till the evolution of ammonia ceases completely (test by bringing a moist red litmus paper near the outlet of the condenser, which will turn blue as long as ammonia is being evolved).
- Titrate the excess of H_2SO_4 against *N*/50 NaOH and note the volume of NaOH used. The end point is reached when the colour changes from pink to yellow.

Observation and Calculation

Weight of the soil sample taken	=	20 g
Volume of *N*/50 H_2SO_4 taken	=	25 mL
Volume of *N*/50 NaOH used (titre value)	=	X mL
Volume of *N*/50 H_2SO_4 consumed for NH_3 absorption	=	(25 – X) mL
1 mL of *N*/50 H_2SO_4	=	0.02 meq / 0.28 mg / 0.0014 g of N
$\therefore$ (25 – X) mL of *N*/50 H_2SO_4	=	0.0014 x (25 – X) g of N
This is present in 20 g of soil		
$\therefore$ in 100 g of soil / % of available N in the given soil sample	=	0.0014 x (25 – X) x (100/20)
Available N in the given soil sample (ppm)	=	0.0014 x (25 – X) x (100/20) x 10000
Available N in the given soil sample (kg/ha)	=	Available N (ppm) x 2.24

Interpretation (Fertility Rating)

Amount of N (kg/ha)	Comments
< 280	Low
280 – 450	Medium
> 450	High

Format of Titration Table

N/50 NaOH Vs *N*/50 H_2SO_4.

S.No.	Aliquot takenin the pipette (mL)	Burette Readings(mL)		Volume of Titrant used (mL)	Indicator	End Point
		Initial	Final			

Things to Learn

1. Why liquid paraffin and glass beads are added during distillation?
2. Can sources of organic matter influence the available N content of soils?
3. Why do we add glass beads while distillation?
4. What is the role of liquid paraffin/paraffin wax in the estimation of N in organic soils?
5. What is the status of available N in Indian soils?
6. How 1 kg/ha = ppm x 2.24?

19

Estimation of Available Phosphorus in Soil

[Bray's Method (Bray and Kurtz, 1945) – Acid Soils]

Introduction

The term available phosphorus (P) refers to the inorganic form, occurring in the soil solution, which is almost exclusively 'orthophosphate'. This orthophosphate occurs in several forms and combinations, and only a small fraction of the total amount present may be available to plants, which is of direct relevance in assessing the P fertility level.

The phosphate concentration in solution is governed by heterogeneous equilibria in which it takes part. This situation can be represented as follows:

P adsorbed in solid phase $\leftrightarrow$ P in the soil solution $\leftrightarrow$ P precipitated

The phosphorus absorbed by plants from soil solution comes from the soil solution in which it exists as inorganic orthophosphate ions *viz.*, $H_2PO_4^-$, HPO_4^{2-} and PO_4^{3-}. The most accessible ion is $H_2PO_4^-$, with the greatest activity coefficient, followed by HPO_4^{2-}. The quantity of P accessible to the plants is influenced by a series of soil properties. The relative abundance of these ions is, however, relatively dependent on the soil pH. For soils having a pH between 4.5 and 7.5, ions of $H_2PO_4^-$ as well as HPO_4^{2-} exist in soil solution. At a pH of 7.2, $H_2PO_4^-$ and HPO_4^{2-} ions have an equal activity, and, when the pH is strongly alkaline (>8.3), ions of HPO_4^{2-} predominate in solution. Above pH of 9.0, the trivalent ion (PO_4^{3-}) becomes more important than $H_2PO_4^-$, but even at a pH of 12, the HPO_4^{2-} concentration is still greater than that of PO_4^{3-}. Soluble phosphorus may be adsorptively retained at the surface of colloidal particles. This retention is more marked when the higher amounts of clay and sesquioxides are present. Relatively, the available inorganic P tends to accumulate in its most stable state under prevailing conditions, thus, in calcareous soils, the available inorganic P would be acid-soluble, whereas, in acid soils the adsorbed P would be more available. In flooded soils, with low oxidation potential, certain forms of P, normally considered as unavailable, for example, iron and phosphate, can be regarded as available. In most soils, the main source of orthophosphate is organic matter unless, of course, direct fertilization, with soluble phosphate, has been made.

Importance

- The available P is considered to be a fairly good indicator / measure of the P supplying capacity of a soil.
- A knowledge of available P content of soils is important for determining its crucial limit, based on soil-test-crop-response calibration study.
- The evaluation of the soil critical limit of P would help in developing P-fertility classes for effective fertilizer recommendation schedule.
- The critical limit of soil P would help eventually in predicting crop response to the applied P.

Principle

This procedure is primarily meant for soils which are moderately to strong acids (pH around 5.5 or less). It has been employed widely to give results that are highly correlated with crop response to phosphate fertilization.

The underlying principle of this method is that the soil is shaken with an extracting solution of 0.03 *N* NH_4F in 0.025 *N* HCl, which dissolves the fractions of P that are considered to be available to plant roots. Ammonium fluoride complexes Al and Fe ions in the acid solution, with the consequent release of P held by the soil, by these trivalent ions. Thus, the combination of HCl and NH_4F helps in removing easily acid–soluble forms of P, largely calcium phosphates, and a portion of the so-called aluminum and iron phosphates.

HCl results in the dissolution of more active calcium, phosphate and, in addition to this, it prevents the precipitation of P (as calcium phosphate), which has been dissolved by ammonium fluoride.

In the filtered extract, P is estimated calorimetrically by adding ammonium molybdate and, thereafter, reducing the molybdenum-phosphate complex with stannous chloride in the acidic medium. The heteropoly complexes (Phosphomolybdates) are formed by coordination of molybdate ions with the P as the central coordinating atom, the oxygen of the Molybdate radicals being substituted for that of PO_4.

The heteropoly complexes, before reduction, give a yellow colour hue to their water solution. In the solution of low P concentration, the molybdate is partially reduced to produce a characteristic blue colour. The intensity, a measure for the concentration of P in the test solution, is read on a Colorimeter.

Reactions

A. Extraction

$3\ NH_4F + 3\ HF + AlPO_4 \rightarrow H_3PO_4 + (NH_4)_3AlF_6$

$3\ NH_4F + 3\ HF + FePO_4 \rightarrow H_3PO_4 + (NH_4)_3FeF_6$

The formulae $AlPO_4$ and $FePO_4$ represent various hydrated and hydroxyl phosphates of Al and Fe, including any adsorbed or precipitated surface layers on oxides of Al, aluminosilicates, and on oxides of Fe.

B. Estimation

$H_3PO_4 + 12\ H_2MoO_4 \rightarrow H_3P\ (Mo_3O_{10})_4 + 12\ H_2O$

(phosphate) (Molybdic acid) (Phosphomolybdate) (Yellow coloured)

Apparatus & Materials Required

1. 100 mL Conical flask
2. 5 mL Pipette
3. 25 mL Volumetric flask
4. 50 mL Measuring cylinder
5. 100 mL Polythene shaking bottle
6. Funnel
7. Whatman No. 42 / 44 filter paper
8. Photoelectric Colorimeter / Spectrophotometer

Reagents Required

1. 1 *N* Ammonium Fluoride (NH_4F) – Dissolve 37.0 g of Ammonium Fluoride in distilled water and dilute the solution to 1 litre and store it in a polythene bottle.
2. 0.5 *N* Hydrochloric acid – Dilute 20.2 mL of Conc. HCl to a volume of 500 mL with distilled water.
3. Extracting solution (Bray No.1 Extractant) – Add 215 mL of 1 *N* NH_4F (37 g of NH_4F is dissolved in 1 litre of distilled water – 1 *N* NH_4F) and 25 mL of 0.5 *N* HCl (20.8 ml of Conc. HCl is diluted to 500 mL with distilled water – 0.5 *N* HCl) to 460 mL of distilled water. This gives a solution composition of 0.03 *N* NH_4F in 0.025 *N* HCl.
4. Dickman and Bray's Reagent-Dissolve 15 g of Ammonium Molybdate (AR grade), $(NH_4)_6Mo_7O_{24}.\ 4H_2O$ in 300 mL of distilled water, warm to about

60°C and filter, if necessary, after cooling. Add to it 342 mL of Conc. HCl and make up the volume to 1 litre. This is 1.5 % solution of Ammonium Molybdate in HCl.

5. Stannous Chloride ($SnCl_2 . 2 H_2O$) solution – Dissolve 10g of Stannous Chloride (AR grade) crystals in 25 mL of Conc. HCl and store in a brown bottle. This is 40% $SnCl_2$ stock solution. A piece of tin metal (AR grade), if added, will keep the stock solution for long.
6. Stannous Chloride working solution-Dilute 0.5 mL of the stock solution to 66 mL with distilled water and prepare this solution just before use.
7. Preparation of standard P solution -Dissolve 0.439 of Potassium Dihydrogen Phosphate (AR grade), KH_2PO_4, in about half a litre of distilled water. Add to it 25 mL of 7 ***N*** H_2SO_4 (approx) and make up the volume to 1 litre with distilled water. This gives 100 ppm stock solution of P. From this prepare a 2 ppm solution by 50 times dilution of the stock solution.

Procedure

A. Extraction

- Weigh 5 g of soil and transfer it to a 100 mL conical flask.
- Add 50 mL of extractant solution to the soil.
- Shake the contents of the flask for exactly 5 minutes, and filter through Whatman No. 42 filter paper. The filtrate should be clear.
- Prepare a blank in which all the reagents are added similarly, except the soil.

B. Estimation (Colorimetry – Dickman and Bray, 1940)

- Take 5 mL of the soil extract as well as different concentration of P (in the range of 0 to 0.8 ppm) by pipetting out 0 (blank), 1, 2, 3, 4, 5, and 10 mL of 2 ppm P solution in 25 mL volumetric flasks.
- Add 5 mL of extracting solution to each of the P standard solution, followed by the addition of 5 mL of Dickman and Bray's reagent in all the flasks (test and P standard)
- To avoid interference of fluoride, 7.5 mL of 0.8 ***M*** boric acid (50 g of H_3BO_3 per litre of distilled water) may be added, if necessary.
- Mix, thoroughly the content of the flasks with about 5 mL of distilled water, washing the neck of the flask down, to remove the adhering ammonium molybdate.

- Finally add 1 mL of working (dilute) stannous chloride solution with immediate mixing, and make upto the mark with distilled water. Once again, mix the solution thoroughly.
- Plot the transmittance readings (% T) of the standards on the ordinate (Y axis) against the concentration in ppm of P on the abscissa (X axis) on a semi logarithmic graph paper for a straight line relationship.
- Measure the intensity of the blue colour just after 10 minutes, in Photoelectric Colorimeter using 660 nm or mm red filter, and adjusting the meter to 100 % transmittance with the blank.
- Determine the concentration of P in the soil extract from the standard curve. This is very important as the colour starts fading after about 15 – 20 minutes of the development of colour.

Observation and Calculation

Weight of the soil sample taken / used in the extraction	= 5 g
Volume of Bray No.1 extractant used for P estimation	= 50 mL
Volume of extract taken for P estimation/colour development	= 5 mL
Final volume made upto	= 25 mL
Transmittance (%) of the test solution (sample)	= T
Concentration of P corresponding to the % transmittance as read from the standard curve	= X ppm
4"Available P in the given soil sample (ppm)	= X x (50/5) x (25/5)
Available P in the given soil sample (kg/ha)	= X x 50 x 2.24
Available P_2O_5 in the given soil sample (kg/ha)	= X x 50 x 2.24 x 2.29

Interpretation (Fertility Rating)

Amount of P (kg/ha)	Amount of P_2O_5 (kg/ha)	Comments
< 11	< 22.5	Low
11 – 22	22.5 – 56.0	Medium
> 22	> 56.0	High

Things to Learn

1. Why Bray method is used to estimate the available P in acid soils?
2. What are the constraints of acid soils in terms of availability of P?
3. What is the status of available P in Indian soils?
4. What do you mean by P fixation?
5. Mention the name of the extractants commonly used for available P estimation.

20

Estimation of Available Potassium in Soil

(Neutral Normal Ammonium Acetate Method)

Introduction

The total potassium (K) content of a soil varies from 0.05 to 2.5 %. The total K is distributed in mineral form (lattice – K, 90-98 %), fixed non-exchangeable or temporarily retrograded K (1-10 %) and exchangeable plus water soluble K (1-2 %). Exchangeable K represents an average of 2 – 15 % of the sum of exchangeable bases and 1 – 3 % of the total capacity for cation exchange. The K concentration in the soil solution is on an average 0.08 – 3 meq/litre. Both water soluble and exchangeable K are most accessible to the plant. Available K can, thus be separated into that, immediately available, which is water soluble and exchangeable, and that, potentially available or fixed. The neutral normal ammonium acetate extract contains both water soluble and exchangeable K. K extraction by this extractant is considered as a suitable index of K availability in most soils, based on crop response correlation study. Thus, the K extracted by this method is equated as the available K.

Importance

- The neutral normal ammonium acetate method does not permit an evaluation of the soil reserves of potassium. Nevertheless, this method characterizes the soil well enough for the momentary state of K supply.
- In order to better know the dynamics of exchangeable K and the supply status of the plant, it is, however, necessary to make two determinations of exchangeable K by the same method at different intervals (at the beginning and during the course of the growth), and draw a curve or balance of their dynamics.
- Very approximately, it may be considered that a good supply of K is available to the plant on a loamy soil, when the exchangeable K represents > 0.25 % of the total K..

Principle

The method is based on the principle of equilibrium of soils with an exchanging cation made of the solution of neutral normal ammonium acetate, in a given soil.

During the equilibrium, ammonium ions exchange with the exchangeable K ions of the soil. The K content in the equilibrium solution is estimated with a Flame Photometer. Since NH_4^+ holds highly charged layers together just as K, the release of the fixed K, in an exchangeable form, is retarded during NH_4OAc extraction.

Reactions

$$\boxed{\text{Clay}} - K + 5\,CH_3COONH_4 \rightleftharpoons \boxed{\text{Clay}} - NH_4 + +5\,CH_3COOK$$

Apparatus & Materials Required

1. 150 mL Conical flask
2. Funnel
3. Beaker
4. Pipette
5. Whatman No. 1 filter paper
6. Shaker
7. Balance
8. Flame Photometer

Reagents Required

1. Neutral *N* Ammonium Acetate (NH_4OAc) solution – Dissolve 77.09 g of NH_4OAc in distilled water and make up the volume to 1 litre. Adjust the solution pH to 7.0, adding acetic acid or NH_4OH solution as required.
2. Potassium Chloride solution – Dissolve 1.908 g of AR grade KCl in distilled water, and make up the volume to 1 litre. It gives 1000 ppm K solution and is treated as stock solution of K.
3. Standard Curve for K (Working K standards) – From the stock solution, take measured aliquots and dilute with NH_4OAc solution to give 10 to 40 ppm of K. After inserting the K filter and regulating the appropriate gas and air pressure, set the Flame Photometer reading at zero for the blank (NH_4OAc solution) and at 100 for 40 ppm of K solution. Draw the calibration curve by plotting the Flame Photometer reading against different concentrations (10, 15, 20, 25, 30, 35, 40 ppm) of K. Any fluctuation in gas and air pressure does not allow steady reading in the meter and must be taken care of.

Procedure

- Weigh 5 g of soil in a 150 mL conical flask.
- Add to it 25 mL of neutral *N* NH_4OAc solution.
- Shake the content of the conical flask on an electric shaker for 5 minutes and filter using Whatman No. 1 filter paper.
- Feed the filtrate into atomizer of the Flame Photometer, 100 of which has been set with 40 ppm K solution and note the reading.
- Locate this reading on the standard curve, which will give the K concentration in the extract.
- From this concentration measurement, the amount of K in the sample is calculated.

Precautions

- The filtrate should be clear. If some soil particles are in the filtrate, it should be re-filtered to avoid the clogging of the suction capillary.
- The air pressure should be between 0.4 and 0.6 kg/cm^2. It should not deviate too much.
- The gas inlet should be opened after opening the air inlet, and closed before shutting off the air supply.
- The flame should be soot-free and blue.
- The Flame Photometer should be warmed up for 10 to 15 minutes before using.

Observation and Calculation

Weight of the soil sample taken	=	5 g
Volume of the neutral *N* NH_4OAc (extractant) used	=	25 mL
Reading of the Flame Photometer for the test solution	=	R
Concentration of K as read from the standard curve	=	C ppm or mg/mL
Therefore in 25 mL of solution	=	C x 25 ppm
This is present in 5 g of soil		
∴ Available K in the given soil sample (ppm)	=	C x (25/5) ppm
Available K in the given soil sample (kg/ha)	=	C x 5 x 2.24
Available K_2O in the given soil sample (kg/ha)	=	C x 5 x 2.24 x 1.20

Interpretation (Fertility Rating)

Amount of K (kg/ha)	Amount of K_2O (kg/ha)	Comments
< 118	< 136	Low
118 – 280	136 – 337.5	Medium
> 280	> 337.5	High

Things to Learn

1. What are the elements that can be estimated using Flame Photometer?
2. What are the soil types in which K availability and fixation are more?
3. What is the status of available K in Indian soils?

21

Estimation of Available Sulphur in Soil

[Williams and Steinbergs (1959) Method]

Introduction

Sulphur (S) occurs in numerous forms in soil, *viz.,* sulphites, sulphates, sulphides and in organic compounds. It is considered that the most accessible form is 'sulphate' (SO_4^{2-}). The organic forms of S compounds become assimilable, especially following, microbiological transformation into SO_4^{2-}. The mineralization of organic S in a soil depends primarily upon the N:S ratio, and any SO_4^{2-} formed may be fixed against extraction, particularly if much Fe or Ba is present or if the soil is very acid. Despite the fact that the plants absorb S almost exclusively as SO_4^{2-}, mobility of SO_4^{2-} in soil may not always yield satisfactory results in accordance with the time of sampling, while assessing SO_4^{2-} availability.

Importance

- Development of chemical test for the estimation of available S (as SO_4^{2-}).is of recent interest in soil testing work, particularly in some reported S deficient areas, and for certain crops, whose requirement of this nutrient is high enough, often, exceeding that of P.
- Of several extracting procedures, suggested for available S determination, starting from distilled water for dissolving out the sulphate form to different chemical extractants *viz.,* Olsen's, Morgan's, Bray's, normal magnesium acetate, 1.0 % NaCl, 0.15 % $CaCl_2$ and phosphate solution.
- For estimating the plant available S in soils, heat soluble S and 0.15 % $CaCl_2$ extractable S methods (Williams and Steinbergs, 1959) are usually recommended.

A. Heat soluble S

Inorganic S (SO_4^{2-}) and a portion of organically held SO_4^{2-}-S are mobilized by special heat treatments and extraction with 1.0 % NaCl. The SO_4^{2-}-S is converted into $BaSO_4$ suspension using $BaCl_2$ crystals and a special conditioning agent. The resulting turbidity is determined by a Spectrophotometer.

Apparatus & Materials Required

1. 10 & 25 mL Measuring cylinder
2. 25 mL Volumetric flask
3. 1 & 5 mL Pipette
4. Erlenmeyer flask
5. Centrifuge tube
6. Reciprocating shaker
7. Water bath
8. Magnetic stirring bar
9. Hot Air Oven
10. Spectrophotometer/Photoelectric Colorimeter

Reagents Required

1. 1.0 % Sodium Chloride (NaCl)-Dissolve 10.0 g of NaCl in 700 mL of distilled water and make upto 1 litre with distilled water.
2. Barium Chloride Dihydrate ($BaCl_2 . 2 H_2O$) crystals (20-30 mesh)
3. Conditioning agent-Dissolve 75 g NaCl in 275 mL of distilled water in a 500 mL volumetric flask, stirring with magnetic stirring bar, add 30 mL of Conc. HCl, 100 mL of absolute ethanol and 50 mL of Glycerol. Rinse Glycerol into flask. Continue stirring until NaCl dissolves. Remove stirring bar and make to volume with distilled water.
4. Standard Sulphate solution-Dissolve 0.5434 g of K_2SO_4 in one litre of distilled water. This contains 100 mg of S per mL of solution. Dilute 10 times to obtain 10 ppm solution. Transfer 0, 5, 10, 15 and 20 mL (equivalent to 0, 50, 100, 150 and 200 mg of SO_4-S) to Erlenmeyer flasks of 150 mL bringing the volume with distilled water to 30 mL.

Procedure

- Weigh 5 g of soil into a silica basin and add 20 mL of distilled water.
- Place the basin on a gently boiling water bath and evaporate to dryness.
- Then, heat it in a hot air oven at 102°C for 60 minutes.
- After cooling, transfer the soil to a 50 mL centrifuge tube and extract it with 33 mL of 1 % NaCl.
- Draw 25 mL of aliquot into a silica basin.

- Evaporate to dryness with 2 mL of 3 % H_2O_2 to remove the interfering organic matter.
- Heat the basin in a hot air oven at 102°C for 60 minutes to remove the excess H_2O_2.
- After cooling, take up the residue in 25 mL water.
- Transfer it to a centrifuge tube and centrifuge to remove the suspended matter.
- Take suitable aliquot and determine the S in it.
- Pipette out 10 or 20 mL of extract in a 150 mL Erlenmeyer flask and add 20 or 10 mL of H_2O_2, thus bringing the volume to 30 mL.
- Add 2.5 mL of conditioning reagent and 0.2 to 0.3 g of $BaCl_2$ crystals by a spatula to the standards and extracts.
- Shake the flasks for one minute each at constant rate.
- After 1 to 3 minutes, measure the turbidity in a Colorimeter using blue filter.
- Turbidity can be more accurately measured at 340 nm on a Spectrophotometer. The turbidity remains constraint for 3 to 10 minutes.

B. $CaCl_2$ Extractable S

In this method, S is extracted with 0.15 % $CaCl_2$ and the soluble sulphate is estimated Turbidimetrically on a Colorimeter using blue filter or Spectrophotometer at 340 nm. In neutral to alkaline soils, 0.15 % $CaCl_2$ may serve as a good extractant as $Ca(H_2PO_4)_2$.

Apparatus & Materials Required

1. 150 mL Erlenmeyer flask
2. Volumetric flask
3. Measuring cylinder
4. Whatman No. 42 filter paper
5. Reciprocating shaker
6. Spectrophotometer / Photoelectric Colorimeter

Reagents Required

1. 0.15 % Calcium Chloride Dihydrate ($CaCl_2 . 2H_2O$) – Dissolve 1.5 g of $CaCl_2 . 2H_2O$ in about 700 mL of water and make up to one litre with distilled water.

2. 1.0 % Sodium Chloride (NaCl)-Dissolve 10.0 g of NaCl in 700 mL of distilled water and make upto 1 litre with distilled water.
3. Barium Chloride Dihydrate ($BaCl_2$. 2 H_2O) crystals (20-30 mesh)
4. Conditioning agent-Dissolve 75 g NaCl in 275 mL of distilled water in a 500 mL volumetric flask, stirring with magnetic stirring bar, add 30 mL of Conc. HCl, 100 mL of absolute ethanol and 50 mL of Glycerol. Rinse Glycerol into flask. Continue stirring until NaCl dissolves. Remove stirring bar and make to volume with distilled water.
5. Standard Sulphate solution-Dissolve 0.5434 g of K_2SO_4 in one litre of distilled water. This contains 100 mg of S per mL of solution. Dilute 10 times to obtain 10 ppm solution. Transfer 0, 5, 10, 15 and 20 mL (equivalent to 0, 50, 100, 150 and 200 mg of SO_4-S) to Erlenmeyer flasks of 150 mL bringing the volume with distilled water to 30 mL.

Procedure

- Weigh 5 g of soil into a 150 mL Erlenmeyer flask.
- Add 25 mL of 0.15 % calcium chloride to it.
- Shake it for 30 minutes on a reciprocating shaker (180 oscillations per minute).
- Filter the suspension through Whatman No. 42 filter paper.
- Analyze 10 to 20 mL of the extract Turbidimetrically as described in the heat soluble S.

Observation and Calculation

Weight of the soil sample taken	= W g
Volume of the aliquot used	= X mL
Volume of the extract prepared	= Y mL
Concentration of SO_4-S corresponding to the % transmittance as read from the standard curve	= C ppm or mg/litre
4-Available sulphur (SO_4–S) present in the given soil sample (mg/kg)	= (C x Y) / (X x W)

Interpretation (Critical levels of Available S for different crops)

Crop	$CaCl_2$ – S (ppm)	Heat soluble – S (ppm)
Rice	10	16
Wheat	13	13
Groundnut	10	11

Things to Learn

1. What is the role of conditioning reagent in the estimation of available S?
2. What is the basic principle involved in Turbidometry?
3. What is the role of H_2O_2 in the estimation of available S?
4. What is the status of available S in Indian soils?
5. Give the various forms of S present in soil.
6. How 1 ppm = 1 mg/litre?

22

Determination of Lime Requirement of Soil

[Shoemaker, Mc Lean and Pratt (SMP) Method, 1961]

Introduction

For proper plant growth, the soil should have a pH between 6.5 and 7.5, though there are certain plants which can grow satisfactorily at low pH, for example, tea, and at high pH, for example, sugar beet. In India, acid soils are located mostly in Eastern, Southern and South Central parts though some soils, at higher elevations, in North India are acidic.

In order to achieve maximum yield and sustained productivity through efficient soil management practices, it is essential to lime an acid soil, as it has considerable influence on soil environment, besides correcting soil acidity.

Several methods have been proposed to determine the lime requirement of acidic soils, to raise the pH around 6.5. The soil pH value alone, however, is not a good criterion for lime recommendation, because of variations in the exchange acidity of soil, and the nature of crops which may not require as high as this pH to produce maximum yield. Of these various methods proposed, the Shoemaker / SMP method was found satisfactory.

The recent trend of liming is to use it as a fertilizer rather than as amendment so as not to disturb heavily the natural environment while ensuring sustained productivity.

Principle

The method involves equilibrating the soil with a pH 7.5 buffer solution, whereby the reserve H^+ is brought into solution, which results in the depression of pH of the buffer solution, a note of which is made and interpreted in terms of the lime required to raise the pH to a desired value.

Apparatus & Materials Required

1. Beaker
2. pH meter

Reagents Required

1. Extractant buffer-Dissolve 1.8 g p-Nitro phenol, 3 g Potassium Chromate, 2 g Calcium Acetate, 53.1 g Calcium Chloride Dehydrate and 2.5 mL Triethanolamine in 1 litre of distilled water, and adjust the pH to 7.5 with NaOH.

Procedure

- First of all determine the pH of the original soil in 1:2.5 soil: water ratio. If the value exceeds 6.0, the method is not applicable to such a soil.
- To maintain 1:2.5 soil:water ratio, take 10 g of soil and add 25 mL of water and stir the suspension for about half an hour.
- If the pH measured, thereafter, happens to be 6.0 or low, then, proceed with the following steps:
- Weigh 5 g of soil in a beaker and add 5 mL of distilled water and 10 mL of the buffer. Stir continuously for 10 minutes or intermittently for 20 minutes.
- Determine the soil pH with the pH meter.
- Lime requirement is done on the basis of soil-buffer pH ready reckoner table given below:

pH of soil buffer suspension	Lime required to bring the soil to indicated pH (tons/acre of pure $CaCO_3$)		
	pH 6.0	pH 6.4	pH 6.8
6.7	1.0	1.2	1.4
6.6	1.4	1.7	1.9
6.5	1.8	2.2	2.5
6.4	2.3	2.7	3.1
6.3	2.7	3.2	3.7
6.2	3.1	3.7	4.2
6.1	3.5	4.2	4.8
6.0	3.9	4.7	5.4
5.9	4.4	5.2	6.0
5.8	4.8	5.7	6.5
5.7	5.2	6.2	7.0
5.6	5.6	6.7	7.7
5.5	6.0	7.2	8.3
5.4	6.5	7.7	8.9
5.3	6.9	8.2	9.4
5.2	7.4	8.6	10.0
5.1	7.8	9.1	10.6
5.0	8.2	9.6	11.2
4.9	8.6	10.1	11.8
4.8	9.1	10.6	12.4

- The values in the table are given in tons of pure $CaCO_3$ per acre, required to bring the soil to the pH indicated, and are required to be converted to their equivalents in the form of agricultural lime to be used.
- For expressing in metric units, i.e., tons per hectare, the figures are to be multiplied by 2.43.

Observation and Calculation

Original soil pH	=	
Soil pH after equilibration with buffer	=	
pH of the soil required to be attained after liming	=	
Amount of lime in terms of pure $CaCO_3$ (tons / acre)	=	
Amount of lime in terms of pure $CaCO_3$ (tons / ha)	=	

Things to Learn

1. What are the liming materials used for acid soil reclamation?
2. What is CCE? Give the CCE for various liming materials.
3. Why the gypsum is not recommended for the reclamation of acid soils?
4. What is neutralizing index?
5. What is the relationship between neutralizing index and neutralizing value?
6. What is the chemical reaction involved in reclaiming the acid soils using lime?

23

Determination of Gypsum Requirement of Soil

[Schoonover (1952) Method]

Introduction

Sodic (Alkali) and Saline-Sodic soils are characterized by the presence of large amounts of sodium, as high as 15% or more, on their exchange complex. As a result of this, the pH of soils increases beyond 8.0, causing nutritional imbalances, elimination of soil organic matter, deterioration of soil physical condition, etc., besides affecting the soil biotic community. Gypsum ($CaSO_4 . 2H_2O$) is commonly used for the management of such soils, when applied in right amounts and size.

Principle

A given weight of soil is equilibrated with a known amount of Ca solution, and the amount of Ca, left in the solution is determined by EDTA titration. The difference between the amount of Ca added and the Ca left in the solution, gives the amount of Ca exchanged. In practice, gypsum of about 1/3 of the value, obtained by this method, is satisfactory in most cases.

Apparatus & Materials Required

1. 50 mL Burette
2. 5 & 100 mL Pipettes
3. 100 & 250 mL Conical flask
4. Filter paper
5. Mechanical shaker

Reagents Required

1. Saturated $CaSO_4$ solution – shake about 5 g of $CaSO_4 . 2H_2O$ with 1 litre of distilled water for 10 minutes, on a mechanical shaker, and filter.
2. Ammonium Chloride Hydroxide buffer – Dissolve 67.5g of NH_4Cl in 570 mL of NH_4OH (specific gravity - 0.86), and dilute to 1 litre.

3. Eriochrome Black-T (EBT) indicator-Dissolve 0.5 g of EBT and 4.5 g of Hydroxylamine Hydrochloride in 100 mL of 95 % ethanol.
4. Standard EDTA solution (0.01 *N*)-Dissolve 2 g of Disodium Dihydrogen-Ehtylene-Diamine-Tetra Acetate and 0.05 g of $MgCl_2$. $6H_2O$ in water, and dilute to 1 litre with distilled water. Standardize the solution against the standard $CaCl_2$ solution.

Procedure

- Weigh 5 g of the processed soil in a 250 mL conical flask, and add 100 mL of the saturated $CaSO_4$ solution.
- Shake for 5 minutes on a mechanical shaker, and filter.
- Pipette out 5 mL of the soil extract into a 100 mL conical flask, and dilute to about 25 mL with distilled water.
- Add 0.5 mL of the NH_4Cl-NH_4OH buffer and 3-4 drops of the EBT indicator.
- Titrate with the standard EDTA solution until the colour changes from wine red to blue.
- Titrate similarly 5 mL of the saturated $CaSO_4$ solution separately.

Observation and Calculation

Weight of the soil taken	=	5 g
Volume of gypsum solution added	=	100 mL
Volume of 0.01 *N* EDTA used for gypsum solution	=	X mL
Volume of 0.01 *N* EDTA used for 5 mL of the filtrate	=	Y mL
Actual volume of 0.01 *N* EDTA used	=	(X – Y) mL
1 mL of 0.01 *N* EDTA	=	0.0002 g of Ca
∴ (X – Y) mL of 0.01 *N* EDTA	=	(X – Y) x 0.0002 g of Ca
This is present in 5 mL of filtrate		
∴ in 100 mL of filtrate	=	(X – Y) x 0.0002 x (100/5) g of Ca
This is present in 5 g of soil		
∴ in 2 million kg of soil	=	(X – Y) x 0.0002 x (100/5) x [(2 x 10^6) / 5] g of Ca
	=	(X – Y) x 1600 kg of Ca / ha
In terms of gypsum requirement	=	1.6 (X – Y) x (172 / 40)
	=	6.88 (X – Y) tons / ha

Things to Learn

1. How will you reclaim the Alkali/ Sodic soils?
2. What is the principle involved in the determination of gypsum requirement?
3. What is the chemical reaction involved in reclaiming the Sodic soils using gypsum?
4. Give the other materials that can be used for the reclamation of Sodic soils.

24

Identification of Some Important Rocks

A. Igneous Rocks

Rocks	Grain Size	Essential Minerals	Most Common Accessory Minerals	Average Specific Gravity	Remarks
Granite	Plutonic Holocrystalline	Predominant Quartz 20 – 35 % Orthoclase	Hornblende Mica Magnetite	2.64	White / Reddish / Blackish
Syenite	Plutonic Holocrystalline	Predominant Quartz 10 % Orthoclase Nepheline Albite	Hornblende Biotite Magnetite	2.80	White / Reddish / Blackish
Granodiorite	Plutonic Holocrystalline	Intermediate Quartz Plagioclase exceeds Orthoclase	Hornblende Biotite Magnetite	2.70	Medium Coloured Reddish
Diorite	Plutonic Holocrystalline	Intermediate Quartz Plagioclase Absent	Hornblende Biotite Magnetite	2.85	Darker
Gabbro	Plutonic Holocrystalline	Labradorite Augite Olivine	Hornblende Illmenite	3.00	Blackish
Dolerite	Hypabyssal Ophitic texture	Labradorite Augite Olivine	Hornblende Illmenite	3.00	Blackish
Basalt	Volconic, Micro crystalline with glassy mass		Hornblende Illmenite	3.00	Blackish

B. Sedimentary Rocks

Name of the Rocks	Mineral Composition	Colour	Structure
Sandstone	Mainly quartz with some cements such as calcium carbonate, iron oxides and clays	Light to red	Usually granular & porous
Shale	Clay minerals, quartz, and some organic matter	Light to dark	Thinly laminated structure
Limestone	Mainly calcite and dolomite with some iron oxides, clay, phosphate and organic matter	Light grey to yellow	Fine grained and compact

C. Metamorphic Rocks

Name of the Rocks	Mineral Composition	Colour	Structure
Gneiss	Formed from Granite, Mineral Composition like that of Granite	Alternating Light and dark	Banded andFoliated
Schist	Formed from Basalt or Shale MineralCompositionmuch as that of original rock	Like original rock	Foliated
Quartzite	Formed from Sandstone and having same composition	Light to brown	Compact and Uniform Non-foliated
Slate	Formed from Shale with same composition as that of original rock	Grey to Black	Compact and Uniform Non-foliated
Marble	Formed from Limestone, consists of mainly calcite and dolomite with minor amounts of pigments such as iron oxides	Light toRed / Green / Black	Compact Fine to Coarse Texture Non-foliated

25*

Identification of Some Important Minerals

*Chapter start from next page

Mineral	Origin	Composition	Colour	Streak	Lusture	Tenacity	Hardness	Specific Gravity
				ELEMENTS				
Sulphur	Secondary	S	Yellow	Yellow to White	Resinous	Translucent	1 – 2	2.07
				OXIDES				
Haematite	Primary / Secondary	Fe_2O_3	Steel	Red	Metallic		5 – 6.5	4.9 – 5.2
Illmenite	Primary / Secondary	$FeTiO_3$	Grey Black	Black	Metallic	-	5 – 6	4.72
Magnetite	Primary / Secondary	Fe_3O_4	Black	Black Metallic	Opaque Metalli	Opaque	5.5 – 6.5	4.9 – 5.2
Pyrolusite	Primary / Secondary	MnO_2	Dark Grey	Black	Metallic	Opaque	6. – 6.5	5.060
Quartz	Primary / Secondary	SiO_2	Various	White	Various	Opaque to Translucent	7	2.6 – 2.7
				HYDROXIDES				
Brucite	Secondary	$Mg(OH)_2$	Greenish White	White	Pearly to Vitreous	-	2.5	2.39
Gibbsite	Secondary	$Al(OH)_3$	Greenish White	White	Pearly to Vitreous	Transparent	2.5 – 3.5	2.4
Limonite	Secondary	$2(Fe_2O_3)$	Yellowish $3H_2O$	Brownish Brown	Earthy Yellow	Opaque	5 – 5.5	3.6 - 4
				SULPHIDES				
Iron Pyrite	Primary / Secondary	FeS_2	Brownish Yellow	Greenish Black	Metallic	Opaque	6 – 6.5	5.01

				SULPHATES				
Gypsum	Secondary	$CaSO_4 \cdot 2H_2O$	White	Greenish White	Vitreous to Pearly	Transparent to Translucent	3.5	2.96
				PHOSPHATES				
Apatite	Primary / Secondary	$Ca_5(PO_4)_3 Fe_2Cl$	Pink to Yellow	White	Vitreous	Transparent	5	3.1 – 3.2
				CARBONATES				
Calcite	Primary / Secondary	$CaCO_3$	Colourless	White	Vitreous	Transparent	3	2.71
Dolomite	Secondary	$CaCO_3$ $MgCO_3$	White	White	Vitreous to Pearly	Transparent	3.5 - 4	2.85
				SILICATES				
				A. Orthoclase Feldspar				
Microcline	Primary Essential	$KAlSi_3O_8$	Grey to pinkish White	White	Vitreous to Pearly	Transparent	6	2.56
Orthoclase	Primary Essential	$KAlSi_3O_8$	Colourless to pinkish White	White	Vitreous to Pearly	Transparent	6	2.56
				B. Plagioclase Feldspar				
Albite	Primary Essential	$NaAlSi_3O_8$	Greyish White	White	Sub Vitreous	Transparent	6	2.6 – 2.7
Anorthite	Primary Essential	$CaAl_2Si_2O_8$	Greyish White	White	Sub Vitreous	Transparent	6	2.6 – 2.78
				MICAS				
Muscovite	Primary Essential	$KAl_2(AlSi_3O_{10})$	Colourless to White	White	Pearly to Vitreous	Transparent	2.5	2.8 – 3.1
Biotite	Primary Essential	$K(Mg, Fe)_3 (AlSi_3OH)(OH)_3$	Brown to dark grey	Grey	Vitreous to Pearly	Transparent	2.5 – 3.0	2.8 – 3.4
				CHLORITE				
Chlorite	Secondary	$Mg_{10}(Al_2Si_6Al_2) O_{20}(OH)_{16}$	Brownish Grey	Grayish White	Earthy to Pearly	Transparent	1.5 - 2.5	2.6 – 3.3

26

Appendices

APPENDIX – I

Guidelines for the preparation of Standard Solution

S.No.	To Prepare 1 litre of 0.1 *N* solution (Approximately)	Standardize with
1.	Sulphuric Acid (H_2SO_4) (Dilute 3.0 mL of Conc. 36 *N* Acid to 1 litre with water)	*N*/10 solution of Na_2CO_3 (5.29 g of A.R. grade dry Na_2CO_3 in water and made up to 1 litre) (or)
2.	Hydrochloric Acid (HCl) (Dilute 10 mL of Conc. 12 *N* Acid to 1 litre with water)	*N*/10 Borax solution [Dissolve 1.907 g of A.R. grade Borax ($Na_2B_4O_7.10H_2O$) in water and make up to 100 mL]
3.	Nitric Acid (HNO_3) (Dilute 6.3 mL of Conc. 16 N Acid to 1 litre with water)	
4.	Sodium Hydroxide (NaOH) (Dissolve 4.0 g in water and make up to1 litre)	*N*/10 solution of Potassium Hydrogen Phthalate ($HKC_8H_4O_4$) (Dissolve 5.1 g of AR Potassium Hydrogen Phthalate in water and Make up to 250 mL) (or) *N*/10 solution of Succinic Acid
5.	Potassium Hydroxide (KOH) (Dissolve 5.7 to 6.0 g in water and make up to 1 litre)	(Dissolve 5.0 g of Succinic Acid in water and make up to 1 litre)
6.	Silver Nitrate ($AgNO_3$) (Dissolve 16.989 g crystalline AR Silver Nitrate in water and make up to 1 litre)	*N*/10 solution of NaCl (Dissolve 5.847 g AR Sodium Chloride in water and make up to 1 litre)
7.	Potassium Dichromate ($K_2Cr_2O_7$) (Dissolve 4.904 g AR Potassium Dichromate in water and make up to 1 litre)	Potassium Dichromate may be used as a primary standard

8.	Potassium Permanganate ($KMnO_4$) (Dissolve 3.25 g Potassium Permanganate in water and make up to 1 litre)	*N*/10 Oxalic Acid {Dissolve 1.574 g pure Oxalic Acid [$(COOH)_2$. 2 H_2O] in water and make up to 250 mL} (or) *N*/10 Sodium Oxalate (Dissolve 1.67 g pure Sodium Oxalate in water and make up to 250 mL)
9.	Sodium Thiosulphate ($Na_2S_2O_3$) (Dissolve 25.0 g pure Sodium Thiosulphate in boiled out distilled water and make up to 1 litre. Add 3.8 g of Borax or 0.1 g of Anhydrous Sodium Carbonate to stabilize the solution)	*N*/10 $KMnO_4$ solution (or) *N*/10 Potassium Iodate (KIO_3) (or) *N*/10 Iodine
10.	Iodine (I) (Dissolve 20.0 g AR Iodate free Potassium Iodide in 30 to 40 mL of water and add 12.7 g sublimed Iodine and make up to 1 litre)	*N*/10 Sodium Thiosulphate ($Na_2S_2O_3$)
11.	Fehling's solution A (Dissolve 69.28 g pure Copper Sulphate ($CuSO_4$) in water and make up to 1 litre) Fehling's solution B [Dissolve 350.0 g Rochelle salt (Potassium Sodium Tartarate) and 100.0 g of Sodium Hydroxide in water and make up to 1 litre]	0.5 % solution of pure AR Glucose (5 mL of Fehling's solution A and 5 mL of Fehling's solution B to titrate against 10 mL of the above standard solution of Dextrose)
12.	Potassium Thiocyanate (KCNS) (Dissolve 10.0 g Potassium Thiocyanate in water and make up to 1 litre)	*N*/10 Silver Nitrate
13	EDTA solution (Dissolve 20.0 g Sodium salt in water and make up to 1 litre)	*N*/10 Calcium solution
14	Ferrous Sulphate (Fe_2SO_4.7 H_2O) (Dissolve 27.8 g in water and make up to 1 litre)	*N*/10 Potassium Dichromate
15.	Ferrous Ammonium Sulphate [Fe_2SO_4 $(NH_4)_2SO_4$. 7 H_2O] (Dissolve 39.2 g Ferrous Ammonium Sulphate in water and make up to 1 litre)	*N*/10 Potassium Dichromate

Annexure–II: Preparation of Standard Stock Solution

Aluminum: Dissolve 1.000 g of aluminum metal in dilute HCl with gentle warming and dilute to 1 liter with reagent water.

Antimony: Carefully weigh 2.743 g of antimony potassium tartrate, $K(SbO)C_4H_4O_6C1/2H_2O$, and dissolve in reagent water. Dilute to 1 liter with reagent water.

Barium: Dissolve 1.779 g barium chloride, $BaCl_2.2H_2O$, analytical grade and dilute to 1 liter with reagent water.

Beryllium: Dissolve 11.659 g beryllium sulfate, $BeSO_4$, in reagent water containing 2 mL nitric acid (conc.) and dilute to 1 liter with reagent water.

Cadmium: Dissolve 1.000 g cadmium metal in 20 ml of 1:1 HNO_3 and dilute to 1 liter with reagent water.

Calcium: Suspend 2.500 g of calcium carbonate, $CaCO_3$, dried for 1 hour at 180°C in reagent water and dissolve by adding a minimum of dilute HCl. Dilute to 1 liter with reagent water.

Chromium: Dissolve 1.923 g of chromium trioxide, CrO_3, in reagent water, acidify (to pH # 2) with redistilled HNO_3 (conc.), and dilute to 1 liter with reagent water.

Cobalt: Dissolve 1.000 g of cobalt metal in 20 ml of 1:1 HNO_3 and dilute to 1 liter with reagent water. Chloride or nitrate salts of cobalt (II) may be used. Although numerous hydrated forms exist, they are not recommended unless the exact composition of the compound is known.

Copper: Dissolve 1.000 g of electrolytic copper in 5 ml of redistilled HNO_3 (conc.) and dilute to 1 liter with reagent water.

Iron: Dissolve 1.000 g iron wire in 10 ml redistilled HNO_3 (conc.) and reagent water and dilute to 1 liter with reagent water. Note that iron passivates in conc. HNO_3, and therefore some water should be present.

Lead: Dissolve 1.599 g of lead nitrate, $Pb(NO_3)_2$, in reagent water, acidify with 10 ml redistilled HNO_3 (conc.), and dilute to 1 liter with reagent water.

Lithium: Dissolve 5.324 g lithium carbonate, Li_2CO_3, in a minimum volume of 1:1 HCl and dilute to 1 liter with reagent water.

Magnesium: Dissolve 1.000 g of magnesium metal in 20 ml 1:1 HNO_3 and dilute to 1 liter with reagent water.

Manganese: Dissolve 1.000 g manganese metal in 10 ml redistilled HNO_3 (conc.) and dilute to 1 liter with reagent water.

Molybdenum: Dissolve 1.840 g of ammonium molybdate, $(NH_4)_6Mo_7O_{24}.H_2O$, and dilute to 1 liter with reagent water.

Nickel: Dissolve 1.000 g nickel metal or 4.953 g nickel nitrate, $Ni(NO_3)_2.6H_2O$, in 10 ml HNO_3 (conc.) and dilute to 1 liter with reagent water.

Osmium: Procure a certified aqueous standard from a supplier and verify by comparison with a second standard. If necessary, standards can be made from osmium compounds. However, due to the toxicity of these compounds, this approach is not advised.

Potassium: Dissolve 1.907 g of potassium chloride, KCl , dried at 110°C, in reagent water and dilute to 1 liter with reagent water.

Silver: Dissolve 1.575 g of anhydrous silver nitrate, $AgNO_3$, in reagent water. Add 10 mL of HNO_3 (conc.) and dilute to 1 liter with reagent water. Store in a dark-colored glass bottle in a refrigerator.

Sodium: Dissolve 2.542 g sodium chloride, NaCl, in reagent water, acidify with 10 ml redistilled HNO_3 (conc.), and dilute to 1 liter with reagent water.

Strontium: Dissolve 2.415 g of strontium nitrate, $Sr(NO_3)_2$, in 10 ml of conc. HCl and 700 ml of reagent water. Dilute to 1 liter with reagent water.

Thallium: Dissolve 1.303 g thallium nitrate, $TlNO_3$, in reagent water, acidify (to pH # 2) with 10 ml conc. HNO_3, and dilute to 1 liter with reagent water.

Tin: Dissolve 1.000 g of tin metal in 100 ml conc. HCl and dilute to 1 liter with reagent water.

Vanadium: Dissolve 1.785 g of vanadium pentaoxide, V_2O_5 , in 10 ml of conc. HNO_3 and dilute to 1 liter with reagent water.

Zinc: Dissolve 1.000 g zinc metal in 10 ml of conc. HNO_3 and dilute to 1liter with reagent water.

APPENDIX – III: Conversion Factors

Non-SI units	Conversion Factor	SI units
Multiply this	**By**	**To obtain this**
Length		
Angstrom, A° (10^{-10} m)	0.1	nanometer, nm (10^{-9} m)
foot, ft	0.304	meter, m
inch, in	25.4	millimeter, mm (10^{-3} m)
micron, m	1	micrometer, mm (10^{-6} m)
mile	1.609	Kilometer, km (10^{3} m)
Mass		
ounze, oz	28.35	grams, g (10^{-3} kg)
pound, lb	453.592	grams, g (10^{-3} kg)
quintal (metric), q	100	kilogram, kg
tonne / ton (metric), t	1000	kilogram, kg
ton (2000 lb), t	907.185	kilogram, kg
Volume		
gallon, gal	3.785	litre, L (10^{-3} m^3)
ounze, fluid, oz	0.03	litre, L (10^{-3} m^3)
cubic foot, ft^3	0.028	cubic meter, m^3
cubic foot, ft^3	28.317	litre, L (10^{-3} m^3)
Area		
acre, ac	0.405	hectare, ha (10^4 m^2)
acre, ac	4046.85	square meter, m^2
Others		
atmosphere	1.013	bar, bar
Bar	100	kilopascal, k Pa (10^3 Pa)
calorie, C	4.19	joule, J
Dyne	5-Oct	newton, N
Erg	7-Oct	joule, J
millimhos/cm, mmhos/cm	1	decisiemen/m, dSm^{-1}
micromhos/cm, m mhos/cm	0.1	millisiemen/m, mSm^{-1}
pound per acre, lb/a	1.121	kilogram per hectare, kg ha^{-1}
pounds per square foot, lb/ft^2	47.88	pascal, Pa
degree Fahrenheit (°F – 32)	0.556	degree Celsius, °C
degree Celsius (°C + 273)	1	Degree Kelvin, K
water potential (mass basis) in bars	100	Joules per kilogram, j kg^{-1}
tons (2000 lb) per acre, t/a	2.242	Metric tons (1000 kg) per hectare, t ha^{-1} (or) Megagrams per hectare, Mg ha^{-1}

millimho per centimeter, mmho cm^{-1}	0.1	Siemen per metre, S m^{-1}
Special Conversions		
P_2O_5	0.44	P
K_2O	0.83	K
MgO	0.602	Mg
CaO	0.715	Ca
P	2.29	P_2O_5
K	1.2	K_2O
Ca	1.39	CaO
Mg	1.66	MgO
ppm	2.24	Kg/ha

* To convert from SI to non-SI units, divide by the conversion factor given

APPENDIX – IV: Some Important Units and Relationships

1 acre	4046.8 m^2
1 hectare	2.471 Acres / 10000 m^2
1 Acre - Inch	3630 ft^3
1 gram	10^6 micrograms / 100 centigrams / 10 decigrams / 1000 milligrams
Parts Per Million (ppm)	mg $litre^{-1}$ / microgram mL^{-1}
milli equivalents	weight in mg / Eq.Weight
1 Siemen	1 mho
1 mmhos cm^{-1}	1 dSm^{-1} or 0.1 Sm^{-1}
1 Bar	0.9869 Atmosphere
1 Atmosphere	33.90 ft of water / 76.0 cm of mercury
1 tonne / 1 Metric ton	1000 kg / 1 Megagram (Mg)
1 meq per 100 g soil	1 centimole per kg of soil
1 meq (K^+) per 100 g soil	10 mmol (K^+) per kg soil
1 meq Ca^{2+} per 100 g soil	10 mmol (1/2 Ca^{2+}) per kg soil /
	10 $mmol_c$ (Ca^{2+}) per kg soil
1 meq Al^{3+} per 100 g soil	10 mmol (1/3 Al^{3+}) per kg soil /
	10 $mmol_c$ (Al^{3+}) per kg soil
CEC (meq per 100 g soil)	CEC (mmols (+) per 100 g soil)
0.1 ***M*** HCl	0.1 mol per litre HCl
1 equivalent of H_2SO_4	1 mole of ½ H_2SO_4 / 1 $mole_c$ of H_2SO_4

APPENDIX – V: Some Prefix, Symbols and Their Meanings

Prefix	Meaning	Symbol	Prefix	Meaning	Symbol
deca	10	da	deci	1-Oct	d
hecta	102	h	centi	2-Oct	c
kilo	103	k	milli	3-Oct	m
mega	106	M	micro	6-Oct	m
giga	109	G	nano	9-Oct	n
tera	1012	T	pico	12-Oct	p
peta	1015	P	femto	15-Oct	f
exa	1018	E	atto	18-Oct	a
zetta	1021	Z	zapto	21-Oct	z
yotta	1024	Y	yocto	24-Oct	y

APPENDIX – VI: Strength of Aqueous Solutions of Some Acid and Aqueous Ammonia

S.No.	Name	Approximate			Volume required to make 1 litre of approximately 0.1 *N* solution (mL)
		Specific gravity	Percentage by Weight	Normality	
1.	HCl	1.18	35	11.3	8.9
2.	HNO_3	1.42	70	16	6.3
3.	H_2SO_4	1.84	96	36	2.8
4.	H_3PO_4	1.69	85	41.1	2.3
5.	CH_3COOH	1.05	99.5	17.4	5.8
6.	Aqueous NH_3	0.9	27.0 (NH_3)	14.3	7.1
7.	H_2O	1	100	-	-

APPENDIX – VII: Choice of Indicators

S.No.	Type of Titration	Example of Reactions	Suitable Indicator	pH range of colour change
1.	Strong Acid Vs Strong Base	NaOH Vs HCl NaOH Vs H_2SO_4 KOH Vs HCL etc.,	Methyl Orange Methyl Red Bromethyl Blue Phenolphthalein	5.0 to 10.0
2.	Strong Acid Vs Weak Base	HCL Vs Na_2CO_3 HCl Vs $NaHCO_3$ HCl Vs $Ca(OH)_2$ H_2SO_4 Vs Na_2CO_3 etc.,	Methyl Orange Methyl Red	4.0 to 6.0
3.	Weak Acid Vs Strong Base	CH_3COOH Vs NaOH CH_3COOH Vs KOH	Phenolphthalein or Thymolphthalein	8.0 to 10.0
4.	Weak Acid Vs Weak Base	CH_3COOH Vs Na_2CO_3 CH_3COOH Vs $NaHCO_3$	No suitable Indicator (Potentiometric titration can be used)	Slow change of pH

APPENDIX – VIII: Properties of Most Important Indicators

S.No.	Name of the Indicator	Colour change		
		Acid	Base	pH range
A. Acid-Base Indicators				
1.	Methyl Violet	Yellow	Blue	0.5 – 1.5
2.	Thymol Blue	Red	Yellow	1.2 – 2.8
3.	Methyl Yellow	Red	Yellow	2.9 – 4.0
4.	Methyl Orange	Red	Yellow	3.1 – 4.5
5.	Bromophenol Blue	Yellow	Bluish Violet	30. – 4.6
6.	Bromocresol Green	Yellow	Blue	3.6 – 5.2
7.	Methyl Red	Red	Yellow	4.2 – 6.3
8.	Bromothymol Blue	Yellow	Blue	6.0 – 7.6
9.	Paranitro Phenol	Colourless	Yellow	6.2 – 7.5
10.	Litmus	Red	Blue	5.0 – 8.0
11.	Phenol Red	Yellow	Red	6.4 – 8.2
12.	Cresol Red	Yellow	Red	7.2 – 8.8
13.	Thymol Blue	Yellow	Blue	8.0 – 9.6
14.	Phenolphthalein	Colourless	Pinkish Red to Pink	8.0 – 10.0
15.	Thymolphthalein	Colourless	Blue	9.3 – 10.5

B. Redox Indicators

S. No.	Name of the Indicator	In (Ox)	In (Red)	E at $H^+ = 1$ (volt)
16.	Methylene Blue	Blue	Colourless	0.53
17.	Diphenylamine	Blue - Violet	Colourless	0.76
18.	Ferroin (Fe^+ ortho phenolphthalein)	Pale Blue	Red	1.14
19.	Neutral Red	Red	Colourless	0.24

C. Miscellaneous

S. No.	Name of the Indicator	Colour change
20.	Potassium Chromate	White to flesh Red
21.	Starch	Colourless to Blue/Blue to Colourless
22.	Potassium Ferricyanide	No Blue Colour/Colourless to brown
23.	Ammonium Purpurate (Murexide)	Colourless to Brown
24.	Erichrome Black T	Purple to Green or Sky Blue

APPENDIX – IX: Average Nutrient Content (%) of Organic Sources

Name	N	P_2O_5	K_2O
Farm Yard Manure	0.85	0.25	0.65
Ground nut cake	7.3	1.5	1.3
Sesamum cake	6.2	2	1.2
Neem cake	5.2	1.1	1.5
Castor cake	4.4	1.1	1.4
Cotton seed cake	4	1.9	1.6
Coconut cake	3	1.9	1.8
Sewage sludge	1.0 – 6.0	0.75 – 2.0	0.4
Dhaincha	3.5	0.6	1.2
Sesbania rostrata	2.8	0.1	1.4
Sunhemp	2.3	0.5	1.8
Composted Coir pith	1.06	0.4	1.2
Fish meal	4	3.9	1.8
Blood meal	10.1	1.2	1
Guano	11	10	2.5
Night soil compost	1.4	2.8	4
Goat manure	2.4	0.9	2
Sheep manure	1.93	1.7	2.3
Pig manure	3.7	3.3	0.4
Poultry manure	2.17	2	4.2
Biogas slurry	1.4	0.9	0.8

APPENDIX – X: Nutrient Content, Moisture, Free Acidity and Equivalent Acidity / Basicity of Nitrogenous Fertilizers

Fertilizer	Formula	N Content				Moisture (%)	Free Acidity (%)	Equivalent Acidity / Basicity	Remarks
		Total	NH_4 - N	NO_3 – N	NH_2 - N				
Ammonium Sulphate	$(NH_4)_2\ SO_4$	20.6	20.6	-	-	1	0.025	110	Sulphur – 24 %
Ammonium Sulphate Nitrate	$(NH_4)_2SO_4 + NH_4NO_3$	26	19.25	6.75	-	1	0.015 (as HNO_3)	93	Sulphur – 15 %
Ammonium Chloride	NH_4Cl	25	25	-	-	2	-	128 - 140	Ca as NaCl – 2 %
Anhydrous Ammonia	NH_3	81.5	81.5	-	-	1	-	148	-
Calcium Ammonium Nitrate	$NH_4NO_3 + CaCO_3$	25	12.5	12.5	-	1	-	Neutral	-
Urea	$CO(NH_2)_2$	46	-	-	46	1	-	80	Biuret – 1.5 %
Ammonium Nitrate	NH_4NO_3	33	16.5	16.5	-	1	-	60	-

APPENDIX – XI: Nutrient Content, Moisture % and Free Acidity of Phosphatic Fertilizers

Fertilizer	Formula	P_2O_5 Content		Moisture (%)	Free Acidity (%)	Remarks
		Water soluble	Total			
Basic Slag	$(CaO)_2.\ (P_2O_5SiO_2)$	-	15.0 – 18.0	-	-	
Rock Phosphate	$[Ca_3(PO_4)_2]_3.\ CaX_2$	-	20.0 – 38.0	-	-	95 % passing in 0.15 mm sieve
Single Super Phosphate	$Ca(H_2PO_4)_2$	16	18.0 – 20.0	12	4 % as P_2O_5	Sulphur – 12 %
Single Super Phosphate	$Ca(H_2PO_4)_2$	16	18.0 – 20.0	5	4 % as P_2O_5	Granulated
Triple Super Phosphate	$Ca(H_2PO_4)_2$	42.5	46	12	3 % as P_2O_5	Sulphur – 1.5 %
Bone meal	$Ca_3(PO_4)_2\ (H_2O)_2$	8	20	8	-	Raw
Bone meal	$Ca_3(PO_4)_2\ (H_2O)_2$	16	22	7	-	Steamed

APPENDIX – XII: Nutrient Content and Moisture % of Potassic Fertilizers

Fertilizer	Formula	Water soluble	Moisture (%)	Remarks
Muriate of Potash	KCl	60	0.5	Sodium as NaCl – 3.5 %
Potassium Schoenite	K_2SO_4. $MgSO_4$. $6H_2O$	23	1.5	Sodium as NaCl – 1.5 %
Sulphate of Potash	K_2SO_4	48	1.5	Total Chloride as Cl – 2.5 % Na as NaCl – 2.0 %

APPENDIX – XIII: Acid Equivalent of Acid forming Fertilizers

Name of the Fertilizers	Acid Equivalent
Ammonium Chloride	128
Ammonium Phosphate	86
Ammonium Sulphate	110
Ammonium Sulphate Nitrate	93
Ammonium Nitrate	60
Urea	80

APPENDIX – XIV: Equivalent Basicity of Basic Fertilizers

Name of the Fertilizers	Equivalent Basicity
Calcium Cyanamide'	63
Calcium Nitrate	21
Dicalcium Phosphate	25
Sodium Nitrate	29

APPENDIX – XV: Ca, Mg and S Content of Some Fertilizer Materials

Name of the Fertilizers	Nutrient Content (%)			
	Ca	Mg	S	Others
Ammonium Sulphate	-	-	24.2	21.0 (N)
Ammonium Sulphate Nitrate	-	-	12.1	26.0 (N)
Basic Slag	33.9	-	3	15.6 (P_2O_5)
Calcium Nitrate	19.4	-	-	-
Copper Sulphate	-	-	11.4	21.0 (Cu)
Elemental Sulphur	-	-	100	-
Ferrous Sulphate	-	-	18.8	32.8 (Fe)
Ferrous Ammonium Sulphate	-	-	16	6.0 (N) 16.0 (Fe)
Gypsum	40	-	23.5	-
Potassium Sulphate	-	-	17.0 – 18.0	48.0 (K_2O)
Potassium Chloride	-	-	-	60.0 (K_2O)
Potassium Magnesium Sulphate	-	11.1	22.3	31.0 (K_2O)
Rock Phosphate	39.0 – 48.0	-	-	25.0 (P_2O_5)
Super Phosphate (Single)	25.0 – 30.0	-	12	16.0 (P_2O_5)
Super Phosphate (Triple)	14.3	-	1	43.5 (P_2O_5)
Urea Gypsum	4.6	-	0.6	36.8 (N)
Urea Sulphur	-	-	10	40.0 (N)
Zinc Sulphate	-	-	17.8	36.4 (Zn)

APPENDIX – XVI: Secondary and Micronutrients Content of Fertilizer Materials

Nutrient	Name of the Fertilizers	Nutrient Content (%)
Calcium	Agricultural Limestone	80.0 – 95.0 ($CaCO_3$)
	Basic Slag	33.9 (CaO)
	Dolomite	20.0 – 45.0 (CaO)
	Gypsum	40.0 (CaO)
	Calcium Ammonium Nitrate	10.0 -20.0 (CaO)
	Super Phosphate (Single)	25.0 – 30.0 (CaO)
	Rock Phosphate	39.0 – 48.0 (CaO)
Magnesium	Magnesium Sulphate	16.0 (MgO)
	Dolomite	5.0 – 20.0 (MgO)
	Magnesite	40.0 (MgO)
	Chelated Magnesium	2.0 – 10.0 (MgO)
Manganese	Manganese Sulphate	30.5 (Mn)
	Chelated Manganese	5.0 – 12.0 (Mn)
Sulphur	Ammonium Sulphate	24.0 (S)
	Super Phosphate (Single)	12.0 (S)
	Potassium Sulphate	17.0 – 18.0 (S)
	Gypsum	13.0 – 18.0 (S)
	Magnesium Sulphate	13.0 (S)
	Iron Pyrites	22.0 – 24.0 (S)
	Ammonium Phosphate Sulphate	15.0 (S)
Molybdenum	Ammonium Molybdate	54.0 (Mo)
Iron	Ferrous Sulphate	20.0 (Fe)
	Chelated Iron (FCO)	12.0 (Fe)
	Chelated Products	5.0 – 10.0 (Fe)
Zinc	Zinc Sulphate	21.0 (Zn)
	Chelated Zinc (FCO)	12.0 (Zn)
	Zinc Sulphate Monohydrate	33.0 (Zn)
Boron	Borax (deca)	11.3 (B)
	Borax (penta)	15.0 (B)
	Boronated SSP	0.18 (B)
	Boric Acid	17.5 (B)
	Solubor	20.5 (B)
Copper	Copper Sulphate	24.0 (Cu)
	Chelated Copper	5.0 – 12.0 (Cu)
Chlorine	Potassium Chloride	48.0 (Cl)